The Year of the Poet XII

June 2025

The Poetry Posse

inner child press, ltd.
'building bridges of cultural understanding'

The Poetry Posse 2025

Gail Weston Shazor
Shareef Abdur Rasheed
Teresa E. Gallion
hülya n. yılmaz
Noreen Snyder
Tzemin Ition Tsai
Elizabeth Esguerra Castillo
Jackie Davis Allen
Mutawaf Shaheed
Caroline 'Ceri' Nazareno
Ashok K. Bhargava
Alicja Maria Kuberska
Swapna Behera
Albert 'Infinite' Carrasco
Kimberly Burnham
Eliza Segiet
William S. Peters, Sr.

~ * ~

In order to maintain each poet's authentic voice, this volume has not undergone the scrutiny of editing. Please take time to indulge each contributor for their own creativity and aspirations to convey their uniqueness.

hülya n. yılmaz, Ph.D.
Director of Editing ~
Inner Child Press International

General Information

The Year of the Poet XII
June 2025 Edition

The Poetry Posse

1st Edition : 2025

This Publishing is protected under Copyright Law as a "Collection". All rights for all submissions are retained by the Individual Author and or Artist. No part of this Publishing may be Reproduced, Transferred in any manner without the prior **WRITTEN CONSENT** of the "Material Owners" or its Representative Inner Child Press. Any such violation infringes upon the Creative and Intellectual Property of the Owner pursuant to International and Federal Copyright Laws. Any queries pertaining to this "Collection" should be addressed to Publisher of Record.

Publisher Information
1st Edition : Inner Child Press
intouch@innerchildpress.com
www.innerchildpress.com

Copyright © 2025 : The Poetry Posse

ISBN-13 : 978-1-961498-66-2 (inner child press, ltd.)

$ 12.99

WHAT WOULD LIFE BE WITHOUT A LITTLE POETRY?

Dedication

This Book is dedicated to

Humanity, Peace & Poetry

the Power of the Pen

can effectuate change!

&

The Poetry Posse

past, present & future,

our Patrons and Readers &

the Spirit of our Everlasting Muse

In the darkness of my life
I heard the music
I danced...
and the Light appeared
and I dance

Janet P. Caldwell

Table of Contents

Foreword .... *ix*

Preface .... *xi*

Emotions .... *xiii*

Love ~ Gratitude ~ Contentment

The Poetry Posse

Gail Weston Shazor	1
Alicja Maria Kuberska	9
Jackie Davis Allen	15
Tzemin Ition Tsai	21
Noreen Snyder	27
Elizabeth Esguerra Castillo	33
Mutawaf Shaheed	39
hülya n. yılmaz	45
Teresa E. Gallion	51
Ashok K. Bhargava	57
Caroline Nazareno-Gabis	65
Swapna Behera	71

Table of Contents ... *continued*

Albert Carassco	79
Kimberly Burnham	83
Eliza Segiet	93
William S. Peters, Sr.	99

June's Featured Poets — 107

Ayham Mahmoud Al-Abbad	109
Til Kumari Sharma	117
Michael Lee Johnson	123
Sylwia K. Malinowska	129

Inner Child Press News — 137

Other Anthological Works — 181

Foreword

Love, Gratitude, and Contentment

Love, gratitude and contentment are the theme assignment for The Poetry Posse.

Love comes in many forms. Love for God and Jesus.. Love for your spouse, your partner, your girlfriend, or boyfriend. Love for your child, parents, siblings and love for your relatives. Love for your friends. Love for all people in this world. Love is universal. Love can change the world.

Gratitude is being grateful for your loved ones and being thankful that you are alive to see another brand new day. Gratitude is being thankful for the smallest, simple things in your life. Being happy, joyful, and bliss. There is always something in your daily life to be thankful for no matter how life can be cruel.

Contentment is having inner peace, and happy with yourself. No one is perfect, and we all make mistakes, yet you are still contented with your life. You are happy and satisfied how far you have come.

In my humble opinion, love, gratitude, and contentment go hand in hand. Put the three together and they can change the world.

Noreen Snyder

Coming Soon

www.innerchildpress.com

Preface

We, **Inner Child Press International, The Year of the Poet** and **The Poetry Posse** welcome you.

As we now are in our 12th year of monthly publications for **The Year of the Poet**, we continue to be excited.

This particular year we have chosen to feature a collection of human emotions. We do hope you enjoy the poet's perspectives on these subjects. Read ~ Learn.

For those of you who are not familiar with our story, back in 2013, a few of us poets got together with the simple intention of producing a book a month. That was our challenge. Since that time the enterprise has blossomed and brought forth a fruit that seems to keep on growing as evidenced as we enter 2023.

Our purpose is simple. Through our lyrical words and verse, we not only wish to share our poetic works, but we also have the poetic naiveté to believe that we can assist in the growth of consciousness of the things that have an effect our collective humanity. Therefore, we welcome your readership. For more about what we are attempting to accomplish, have a look at our Publishing Web Site . . . www.innerchildpress.com. If you would like to

know a bit more about this particular endeavor please stop by for a visit at :
www.innerchildpress.com/the-year-of-the-poet

Over the years, Inner Child Press has been socially active to bring awareness and catalog through literature the things that have an impact upon our world and its inhabitants. We have solicited, produced, underwritten and published quite a few volumes to that end. For more insight you may wish to visit : www.innerchildpress.com/the-anthology-market. If you are a writer, poet, or activist, you would be advised to keep a eye out for upcoming volumes should you desire to participate. All readers are welcomed as well. Note, that there is a myriad of published volumes that are available as a FREE PDF download as well as available for purchase at affordable prices.

We at this time extend to you our well wishes for your own personal journey and hope that you consider including us as a travel companion.

Bless Up

Bill

William S. Peters, Sr.

Publisher
Inner Child Press International
www.innerchildpress.com

Love ~ Gratitude ~ Contentment

Love	Gratitude	Contentment
Red Roses	Blue Hydrangea	Azure Bluets

In 'All I Cannot Save,' Adrienne Rich portrays all the creatures she loves. "My heart is moved by all I cannot save, so much has been destroyed. I have to cast my lot with those, who, age after age, perversely, with no extraordinary power, reconstitute the world."

Gratitude and contentment often accompanies awareness of what we are lucky to have in our world. Sometimes what we have is huge, beautiful, or amazing. Often it is the little things, the small joys that make for a wonderful life. Alison Luterman in 'Consider the Generosity of a One-Year-Old' writes, "If you were outdoors she would hand you a dead beetle, a fistful of grass, a pebble, by way of introduction or just because. And if, a moment later, she wants it back, it would be for the joy of passing these simple symbols back and forth, freely offered, freely relinquished, This is me. Here is who I am."

In this volume of 'The Year of The Poet,' we share who we are right now, right here, and what we love or are grateful for, as well as what brings us contentment and all the things that make life meaningful. Our themes for this book are Love, Gratitude, and Contentment.

We offer up the stuff that we appreciate, each in our own unique way. As Barbara Crooker says in 'Praise Song,' "Praise the meadow of dried weeds: yarrow, goldenrod, chicory, the remains of summer. Praise the sun slipping down behind the beechnuts. Though darkness gathers, praise our crazy fallen world; it's all we have." What do you see around yourself that should be praised?

Each of the poets have focused on some aspect of their lives, bringing forth a cacophony of meaning and showing us that we all love and appreciate in our own way, making way for each person's way of loving the world. What do you enjoy and value about your world?

Really look around, as Roger S. Keyes encourages "Hokusai says look carefully. He says keep looking, stay curious. He says there is no end to seeing. He says look forward to getting old. Don't be afraid. Look, feel, let life take you by the hand."

Do you look forward to getting old? Explore what you look forward to. What message is the world giving you right now?

Kimberly Burnham

Integrative Medicine
Spokane Washington

Poets . . .
sowing seeds in the
Conscious Garden of Life,
that those who have yet to come
may enjoy the Flowers.

Poets, Writers . . . know that we are the enchanting magicians that nourishes the seeds of dreams and thoughts . . . it is our words that entice the hearts and minds of others to believe there is something grand about the possibilities that life has to offer and our words tease it forth into action . . . for you are the Poet, the Writer to whom the Gift of Words has been entrusted . . .

~ wsp

poetry is . . .

Poetry succeeds where instruction fails.

~ wsp

Coming Soon . . .

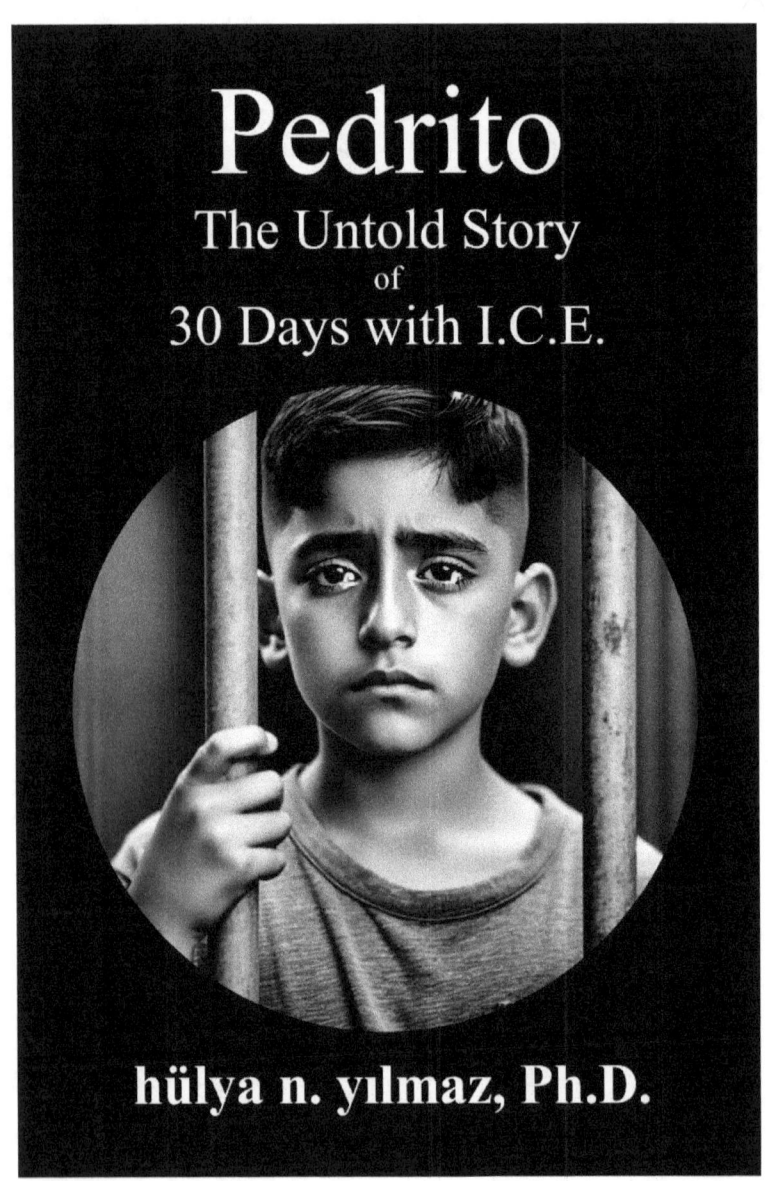

Gail Weston Shazor

Gail Weston Shazor

Gail Weston Shazor is a lover of words. She is fond of the arcane, unusual and the not yet words.

Coining words at an early age, there was often a bit of trouble with teachers, but she always had her mother and aunt to back up her choices in expression. Born in Mississippi, she spent her early years with her grandparents. Each of the four left very careful influences on her pre-schooling. She learned in turn how women worked in and out of the home and how men worked in and out of the home to support the family. She learned that a lack of proper schooling was not the only way to learn and understanding life was a great teacher. As in most rural families of color, women had a greater chance of formal learning. Both of Gail's grandmothers read out loud to the family whether it was the bible or the newspapers and important documents to their spouses.

Gail Weston Shazor has authored (so far) Notes from the Blue Roof, A Overstanding of an Imperfect Love, HeartSongs and Lies My Grandfather's Told Me. The number of anthologies is too many to list with the premier accomplishment of one of the contributors to The Year of The Poet. Gail will always lend her ink to community projects and will purchase the books of fellow poets in the Inner Child Press family.

Emancipation

I lost the title in my thoughts
So jumbled together as they were
Fleeting around the edges
Of memories, old, new and coming
Gone are the days
That we separated each other
By skin color
And when my generation dies
You will have to find colorism in a book
There is no forbidden love
No love that we have to be jailed for possessing
I can remember being bi-colored
High Yellow
Mullato
Mixed Race
And I only think on bears now
Would I fear a polar bear more than a brown bear?
Are my white relatives to be feared
More than my black or
My Indian tribe,
I don't think so
I wonder if sisters on each side
Of the Berlin Wall would genetically change
To enemies
Or did the Tutsis gain education because
They favored the Belgians more in complexion
Than the Hutus
All sharing a common language
For thousands of years with the TWA people
Why is a house slave better
Then a yard slave
Or a field slave
800,000 rumors on African soil
1 little girl on Mississippi soil
Who has never seen a bear free

The Year of the Poet XII ~ June 2025

Taught that life labeled dangerous
Had to be caged
And still clinging to the thought
Of Native ancestors that all life
Is cherished life
I drink water now
And ponder on the life that calls to me
From the margins
Jumbled together as they are
Whispering to be heard
This started as a Happy Mother's day piece
And so it goes
All women are wisdom bearers
And they exist to share the knowledge
Whether actively birthing or not
As they teach the children
All children
To see life
Question life
And protect life
So bears can continue to exist
Free
So we can continue to exist
Without labels
Free

Carnival!

The day was warm and festive
And while I stood
Anticipatingly
Alongside the side of the road
I watched the kids
Mimicking my impatience
Stepping from foot to foot
Fanning the heat away from my face
Looking down the street

We could hear them all
The steel drums
And brown arms rocking the frames
So tenuously attached to parents
I smile at the younger me-s
Knowing that very soon
Happy will burst across our faces
At the first site of
Color
Color intertwined with
Swaying hands
And wind driven movements
Inviting us to join in the dance
Us wishing we had feathers
And sparkling shoes to step
Away from our drab lives in

The island shook under the vibration
Of so many souls at play
The watching and the watched
Plumed for the day in the rhythm
Of Carnival

7 cubed religion

Palm Sunday now has come and gone
Where should I be on my road?
The one that leads to freedom
Or at least to forgiveness
Isn't that what we practice
During this week called "holy"
Maybe it just takes me to church

The store full of frock buyers
Searching for the perfect hat
To match the shoes that you found
And the fun house mirrors swirl
Until even the devilish
Faces in the regular pews
Can be made to look pretty

We greeted others with hugs
And then a kiss for each cheek
I check for the smear of paint
On the inner palm of hands
Maybe new paint since Sunday
After the promise of palms
May have moved you to action

Greet me with Jesus loves me
Jesus fed the multitude
With what will you nourish me
Have your hands become dirty
Will you stand with while I cry
Wipe my tears with your satin
Or have your eyes become blind

Abba Father, You are Lord
But whom do You so favor
I used to be a Baptist

Gail Weston Shazor

I used to be Methodist
Now I just want to be yours
Find in me a wildling heart
Free me from the lock of bricks

The world is moaning loudly
And the jews are down the street
And the gentiles are there too
And everyone closes doors
Their religion is now safe
From the ones who need the Christ
And the church people sing loud

Spending this easter morning
Where land parted from water
And altars grow in desserts
And the sap runs loud in trees
I will wait for Him outside
With my hands dirty of love
Doing, cause He said to go

Alicja Maria Kuberska

Alicja Maria Kuberska

Alicja Maria Kuberska – awarded Polish poetess, novelist, journalist, editor.

She is a member of the Polish Writers Associations in Warsaw, Poland and IWA Bogdani, Albania. She is also a member of directors' board of Soflay Literature Foundation, Our Poetry Archive (India) and Cultural Ambassador for Poland (Inner Child Press, USA)

Her poems have been published in numerous anthologies and magazines in : Poland, Czech Republic, Slovakia, Hungary,Ukraina, Belgium, Bulgaria, Albania, Spain, the UK, Italy, the USA, Canada, the UK, Argentina, Chile, Peru, Israel, Turkey, India, Uzbekistan, South Korea, Taiwan, China, Australia, South Africa, Zambia, Nigeria

She received two medals - the Nosside UNESCO Competition in Italy (2015) and European Academy of Science Arts and Letters in France (2017). Ahe also received a reward of international literary competition in Italy „ Tra le parole e 'elfinito" (2018). She was announced a poet of the 2017 year by Soflay Literature Foundation (2018).She also received : Bolesław Prus Prize Poland (2019), Culture Animator Poland (2019) and first prize Premio Internazionale di Poesia Poseidonia- Paestrum Italy (2019).

Love

Love me unconditionally.
For you I will be
Water, air
The sun, the moon,
And the stars in the sky.
See me
The same way always.
Do not heed the years,
The first grey hair
And the wrinkles under the eyes.
You know
That when the body ages
The soul stays young.
The interior radiates beauty.
Love me for being me.

Far Happiness

Happiness needs very little space
- a house with a family, a garden
and several adjacent streets are enough.

It likes to sleep in the shade of trees,
wrap itself in the aroma of flowers,
talk to bees about the hardships of life
and echo birds in singing.

It floats in the aromas of baking,
hides in a piece of fresh bread
and bubbles in a cup of milk.

Sometimes it picks ripe apples in the orchard,
spits cherry seeds at a distance,
peeps into the pots in the kitchen,
stirs a spoon on a plate with some soup.

It laughs loudly or giggles softly,
dances and jumps up and down
humming favorite songs.

From time to time it flies kites,
plays football with children,
hugs its favorite teddy bear
at bedtime

In a refugee camp,
in the crowded tents
there is no place for happiness.

Stubborn – it returns in dreams
and like an echo
reminds of the good times.
The longing calls for return
to its homeland.

Alicja Maria Kuberska

The Islands of Happiness

dreams come true in the Bahamas

let's go there
where the wind brushes the green hair of palm trees
the huge ocean murmurs sleepily
the golden sand remembers footprints
and the sun disappears in blue water in the evening

before the black butterfly appears
we have time to write a few lines of a poem
and to share our thoughts like a slice of bread

only there
we can entrust our secrets to the stars

Jackie Davis Allen

Jackie Davis Allen

Jackie Davis Allen, otherwise known as Jacqueline D. Allen or Jackie Allen, grew up in the Cumberland Mountains of Appalachia. As the next eldest daughter of a coal miner father and a stay at home mother, she was the first in her family to attend and graduate from college. Her siblings, in their own right, are accomplished, though she is the only one, to date, that has discovered the gift of writing.

Graduating from Radford University, with a Bachelor's of Science degree in Early Education, she taught in both public and private schools. For over a decade she taught private art classes to children both in her home and at a local Art and Framing Shop where she also sold her original soft sculptured Victorian dolls and original christening gowns.

She resides in northern Virginia with her husband, taking much needed get-aways to their mountain home near the Blue Ridge Mountains, a place that evokes memories of days spent growing up in the Appalachian Mountains.

A lover of hats, she has worn many. Following marriage to her college sweetheart, and as wife, mother, grandmother, teacher, tutor, artist, writer, poet and crafter, she is a lover of art and antiques, surrounding herself, always, with books, seeking to learn more.

In 2015 she authored *Looking for Rainbows, Poetry, Prose and Art*, and in 2017, *Dark Side of the Moon*. Both books of mostly narrative poetry were published by Inner Child Press and were edited by hulya n. yilmaz in 2019, *No Illusions. Through the Looking Glass*, which was nominated to be considered for a Pulitzer Prize by the publisher and editor of Inner Child Press, ltd.

http://www.innerchildpress.com/jackie-davis-allen.php
jackiedavisallen.com

Jackie Davis Allen

Gratitude

As a young girl, a teen,
What passed for love, really wasn't.

Tender in years, experience lacking,
Words unable to confess until
Multiple Heart's-aches had healed.

As an older teen, determined, I grew
With hindsight of knowledge,

A child's understanding of Puppy Love.
Increased emotions, highly charged them.
Time and age transform youthful sentiments.

Anger, resentment, and hurt fade, turn
Into gratitude for the greater good.

Love's reciprocal relationship
Ensues with age, eventually. It must!
Thanks be to God.

Adolescent entanglement left behind,
Experience now offers up possibilities.

Commitment

Getting to know you,
Getting to love you,
I stumbled over the building blocks
Of Puppy Love, and adolescent expectations.

I nursed my aches, attempted
To soothe my pains.
With new and varied experiences,
Time became my friend.

Healing from past bruises,
I nursed my wounds; my eyes cleared.
My heart accepted the need
To be true to myself.

And then, true love appeared.
Accepting, not rushing,
Taking care to know each other,
We're grown stronger, closer with the years.

Jackie Davis Allen

Love

I'm in love, for the very first time,
No pretense, no need to pretend
That I am anything other than what I am.

Free, free, at last, no make-up required
To notice the bee to my flower,
As one, we're in a symbiotic relationship.

I'm in love, I'm in love,
Though the years have turned my hair
A shade of whitish-gray.

My waistline has expanded,
So too the numbers of our family;
Of our years together, more than a half-century.

From riding the high waves
Of our fresh, abiding love, now
We bask contentedly in each other.

From the mountains to the valleys,
From the skies to the seas,
As best friends, love binds us together.

Tzemin Ition Tsai

Tzemim Ition Tsai

Dr. Tzemin Ition Tsai comes from the Republic of China(Taiwan). In addition to being a professor of literature at a university, he is more committed to writing poems, novels, and proses. He is also an editor of "Reading, Writing and Teaching" academic text, an International editor of "Contemporary dialogues" literary periodical in Macedonia, and Vice-Chairman of the International Jury of the SAHITTO INTERNATIONAL AWARD in Bangladesh, and a columnist for "Chinese Language Monthly" in Taiwan.

In a wide range of literary creations, he is particularly fond of interesting stories or novels, and writing articles or poems about the feelings of nature and human beings. He has won many national literary awards. His literary works have been anthologized and published in books, journals, and newspapers in more than 55 countries and have been translated into more than 24 languages.

Tzemim Ition Tsai

I Carry Your Yes

I carry your yes like rain that never falls,
Yet floods all my smallest silences.
The world—blue, green, hushed—leans
When you whisper me.
I become a candle dancing
In the grammar of your hands.
No map, no moon could ever
Unkiss this gravity.
Even stars, those well-behaved punctuation marks
Of the night, blink
When you pass.
You rearranged the sky inside me—
Moved constellations I didn't know I kept.
Love is not a song,
It is the voice beneath the voice,
The pause between the chords,
The breath before the name.
I would build a house out of your laughter
If wind permitted.
I would trade every alphabet I know
For the single touch
Of your unspoken syntax.
And when I sleep,
The dream wears your face
But never calls itself a dream.

The Old Barrow

I followed the furrow where the barrow once stood,
Its handles weathered thin as my father's knuckles—
Oak-smoothed, and blessed by callus and time.
He wheeled it like a prayer through loam and clover,
Spilling seed with every turn of breath.
The wind is honest here, still full of him.
It hauls old names from hedgerows and fieldstone.
I hear them creak beneath the boots of dusk,
Along paths worn thinner than his Sunday shirt.
When I stoop to gather the broken ploughshare,
Rusted red as a robin's breast in March,
I know the earth remembers everything—
And I am grateful it forgets nothing.

Laundry Day in April

My neighbor folds shirts
with the same reverence
others reserve for prayer.
She lifts a sleeve,
smooths it like an old sorrow
that no longer needs words.
We do not speak of money,
or fame,
or what didn't happen.
Instead, she hands me a fig
from her backyard tree,
and says,
"It is enough this year
they didn't fall before ripening."
The cat sleeps under the laundry line.
A plane passes overhead,
but no one looks up.
Somewhere, someone wants more.
Here, we sit on cracked steps
and sip tap water
as if it were holy.
The sun drapes itself across the fence,
not asking anything.

Noreen Snyder

Noreen Snyder

Noreen Ann Snyder has been writing since she was a teenager. She writes a variety of different topics. Her favorite poetic forms are Sonnets, Blitz, Haiku, Tanka, and Free Verse. She always learning different poetic forms.

Noreen Ann Snyder is a poet, writer, and an author of five books, (four books are co-authored with her late husband, Garry A. Snyder.) Her poetry is in several Inner Child Press Anthologies. She is the founder ofThe Poetry Club on Facebook.

Noreen Snyder

Being in Love

To love and to be loved back
by a special person
like walking through a field
of daisies with the breeze
hitting me gently.
If I could, I would walk up
to the nearest cloud and
shout, "I'm still in love with
my Teddy Bear Darling and he's
in love with me too.
I want people to experience
what it's like being in love.
Oh, what a bliss, joy, and happiness

Gratitude

At 67 I'm thankful for waking up
each morning, being able to touch
the floor with both feet and
standing up without any help.

Making my own coffee
and drinking my delicious coffee.
Being able to cook my own meals
without problems.

Being able to read a good book or
a magazine and writing poetry,
and being involved in
the poetry community.

Being able to inhale and exhale air
without any oxygen tank.
Walking outside to feel the breeze
or the hot sun against my flesh.

I don't know how long I have on this Earth,
but I'm eternally grateful to God for
keeping me alive and allowing me to
see another beautiful day.

Noreen Snyder

Contentment (Haiku)

Having inner peace

and satisfied who you are

and where you're going

Elizabeth E. Castillo

Elizabeth Esguerra Castillo

Elizabeth Esguerra Castillo is a multi-awarded and an Internationally-Published Contemporary Author/Poet and a Professional Writer / Creative Writer / Feature Writer / Journalist / Travel Writer from the Philippines. She has 2 published books, "Seasons of Emotions" (UK) and "Inner Reflections of the Muse", (USA). Elizabeth is also a co-author to more than 60 international anthologies in the USA, Canada, UK, Romania, India. She is a Contributing Editor of Inner Child Magazine, USA and an Advisory Board Member of Reflection Magazine, an international literary magazine. She is a member of the American Authors Association (AAA) and PEN International.

Web links:

Facebook Fan Page

https://free.facebook.com/ElizabethEsguerraCastillo

Google Plus

https://plus.google.com/u/0/+ElizabethCastillo

Elizabeth Esguerra Castillo

Flight of Love

In the quiet glow of evening light,
Two hearts converge, their spirits bright.
With every whisper, with every sigh,
Love takes flight, like a soft lullaby.

Hand in hand, through paths we roam,
In every smile, we find our home.
Contentment blooms in the simplest things,
Like laughter shared and the joy it brings.

The warmth of your touch, a reassuring grace,
In your embrace, I find my place.
The world may rush, but here we stand,
In this moment, perfectly planned.

Melodies of life play sweet and low,
In the garden of love, our hearts will grow.
With every dawn, we'll start anew,
In a dance of dreams, just me and you.

So let us cherish what we have found,
In love's gentle arms, forever bound.
Contentment lives in the little things,
In every heartbeat, our happiness sings.

Empath

In quiet corners of the heart,
An empath weaves, with gentle art,
A sorrow shared, a joy expressed,
With open arms, we are caressed.

They walk with shadows, feel the light,
In every laugh, in every fight,
A mirror held to souls in pain,
With whispered kindness, healing rain.

A tender touch, a knowing glance,
In the chaos, they find the dance,
They hold our stories, large and small,
And catch the tears when raindrops fall.

Though heavy is the weight they bear,
Their spirit shines, with love to share,
In every heartbeat, every sigh,
An empath's gift is to empathize.

With thread of gold, they weave the night,
Transforming darkness into light,
And in their presence, hearts expand,
As they embrace us, hand in hand.

Elizabeth Esguerra Castillo

Gentle Soul

In the stillness of the dawn,
A gentle stir begins to rise,
From shadows deep, the light is drawn,
As dreams dissolve and hope complies.

Awakened soul, embrace the day,
Leave behind the veil of night,
With open heart, let worries sway,
And find your path, illuminated bright.

Each breath a promise, fresh and new,
As whispers chase the fading stars,
The world awaits your vibrant hue,
A canvas wide, no walls, no bars.

In quiet moments, hear the call,
The melody of life unfolds,
Stand tall, for you can have it all,
A tale of courage yet to be told.

So rise, dear soul, and take your flight,
Into the arms of morning's grace,
For in your heart, a spark ignites,
An awakened journey, time to chase.

Mutawaf Shaheed

Mutawaf Shaheed

C. E. Shy has been writing since the seventh grade. He continued writing through high school, until he became more involved in sports. After his graduation, he worked at the White Motors Company where he wrote for the company's newspaper. He started a column called: "The Poet's Corner." That was his first published work.

www.innerchildpress.com/c-e-shy.php

Did You Forget?

Exercise then rest. Breakfast brunch.
I never look for inspiration it usually
find me when I'm looking.

There are certain sounds that bring it
around. I try to attract it sometimes
sometime it works. Avoiding jerks,
works really well.

Too much passion is like too much wine.
Making love is like drinking water, one cup
is not enough. I'm grateful though!

Oh, by the way this is the last day of summer.
Or did you forget in the midst of our slumber?

Red Lined

At night I write fulfilling my pens appetites.
When I sleep it puts red ink on my dream. It
tells me to say to the dream, "I'll see you later."
The light is too bright, so record it on my phone.

It was hard to record my wins and losses. I am
satisfied with being balanced. Every now and
then I worry over words that get lost along the
way, trying to find my pens mind.

There are words, when found the only thing you
can do is scribble and figure out later what
the heck was said. Go on write them down.

I laugh when I remember the paragraphs that were
driven by cups of coffee. The batteries are low and
I have to go. The dream that was postponed is still
there waiting.

While We Can

Hey grandson walk come with
me while we can, talk with me
while you can.

I may be able to point out some
things you don't see. I can tell
you some stuff you don't understand.

I will give you some knowledge
that will put out front of the
crowd.

I'll show a way you can side step
trouble and stay   out of jail, to
keep your parents from posting
a bail.

I know right now you think you
know. If you take this walk with
me, you'll see you don't.

If you apply what I teach, you may
survive. Asking your friends, don't
bother, until they take a walk with
their grandfather.

hülya n. yılmaz

hülya n. yılmaz

Liberal Arts Professor Emerita, hülya n. yılmaz [sic] is Co-Chair and Director of Editing Services at Inner Child Press International, a published author, ghostwriter, and translator (EN, DE, and TU; in any direction). Her literary contributions appeared in a large number of national and international anthologies.

hülya writes creatively to attain and nourish a comprehensive awareness for and development of our humanity.

hülya n. yılmaz, a traveler on the journey called "life" . . .

Writing Web Site
https://hulyanyilmaz.com/

Editing Web Site
https://hulyasfreelancing.com

infinite love

i may have been 10 or 11
a classmate was passing around a notebook
"write in here what you think 'love' is," she said

a lifetime has passed since that day's recess
i remember how awkward i felt, though - trying to define
"love"
and want to hope that my words have never made it out of
that page

"love" cannot be defined; it must be experienced, lived
as i have before, during and after the birth of my One and
Only,
my daughter of physical beauty, coupled with an all around
beauty

another lifetime went by, with my precious child by my
side
then came her time to be a mother - a magnificent Mom, at
that
first, a boy and less than 2 years later, a girl

i have now entered my final lifetime
surrounded by the love of my 3 true gems
and my love for each one of them

"love" being experienced, lived

how not to confine "gratitude"

have you ever felt so grateful
that your heart started to beat faster
your eyes sparkled out of their sockets
your mouth dried up like parchment paper
your feet picked up their speed to a solo dance
your voice, in a soft whisper at first, rose to the sky
and composes its unique melody

"thank you, Universe
thank you for letting me be one with you!"

the homeless man

one cardboard
one torn blanket
two hole-filled socks
only one shoe
a scruffy dog
being fed scraps
scraps he had found
in a trash bin on an alley

curious, the child passing by
with his mother, asked:
"why don't you eat the scraps?"
"i had an apple core this morning
but my loyal partner was without food
since yesterday. So, it's his turn now."

Teresa E. Gallion

Teresa E. Gallion

Teresa E. Gallion is a seeker on a journey to work on unfolding spiritually in this present lifetime. Writing is a spiritual exercise for Teresa. Her passions are traveling the world and hiking the mountain and desert landscapes of the western United States. Her journeys into nature are nurtured by the Sufi poets Rumi and Hafiz. The land is sacred ground and her spiritual temple where she goes for quiet reflection and contemplation. She has published five books: Walking Sacred Ground, Contemplation in the High Desert, Chasing Light, a finalist in the 2013 New Mexico/Arizona Book Awards, Scent of Love, a finalist in the 2021 New Mexico/Arizona Book Awards and Come Egypt in 2024. She has two CDs, *On the Wings of the Wind* and *Poems from Chasing Light*. Her work has appeared in numerous journals and anthologies.

Website: http://teresagallion.yolasite.com/

Teresa E. Gallion

Grateful Heart

The morning glows below a blue sky.
A breeze whispers across the patio.
Gratitude slaps me from cheek to cheek
as a spring breeze serenades my ears.

The smile on my face may be contagious.
Love wants to explode from my heart
and hug you beyond human emotion.
The morning melody is a gentle touch.

It lingers like a soothing massage,
softly teasing a grateful soul.
If I go to sleep, do not awaken me
from this joyful noise.

Gratitude will carry me
where I need to be.
Sitting with love and laughter
at the Beloved's feet.

A Thousand Steps

Love is a thousand steps plus one.
Let us start walking now
to get ahead of those billion lanterns
lighting up the sky.

You are my anchor
as I walk this pathway.
I will only be afraid,
if I cannot feel your presence.

I am bound to your commitment
to stay close to me
through all the shadows
and valleys that burn.

The pulse of the Infinite
hugs the chambers of my soul.
I feel one with the undefinable
spark of light from Spirit.

A symphony of silence touches me.
I want to Dance with the light,
embrace the sound current
and feel love flow through me.

Breathe Contentment

Contentment is like a giggling river
happily running in the water.
It is the cousin to a field of daisies
swaying in the wind.

It does not promise anything.
It simply touches you deeply,
catches you dancing with daisies
and giggling from deep within.

Contentment is a captured moment
that holds the soul tight.
You open your eyes wide
and float in a river of bliss.

Ashok K. Bhargava

Ashok K. Bhargava

Ashok Bhargava is a poet, writer, inspirational speaker and a literary consultant. He has attended poetry conferences in Italy, Turkey, India and Philippines. His latest book "Riding the Tide" about his battle with cancer has been translated and published in Arabic, Hindi, Telugu and Bengali languages. He is a contributing writer to several anthologies worldwide including World Poetry Almanac 2014. He has been published in numerous print and online magazines.

Ashok has won many accolades including Poet Ambassador to Japan, Kalidasa International award, World Poetry Lifetime Achievement award, Writers Beyond Borders Peace award and Tapsilog Leadership award for his community involvement. He is founder of Writers International Network Canada Society to discover, nourish, recognize and celebrate writers, poets and artists and to assist them to network with the community at large. He is the author of eight books of poetry and one anthology. He is Artist-in-Residence at Moberly Arts & Cultural Centre and also co-edits the literary section of The Link Newspaper.

My Secret Garden

Morning sky promises
glossy pink
color of the sunshine
and a brand new
yellow-green sprout
a taste of honesty
continuity
brevity
precision
beauty
born after yesterday's harvest
that hints
the secret of reincarnation
while fingers snap
a newly formed bean.

After watering
I become air
invisible.

Flowers dance
with the words
life is for sowing
not the expectation of harvest.

The past has its own predicaments
for the future happiness
there is pain in being ignored
the way eyes look back.

So much good so much bad.
It is the bad we remember
to replace one negativity with another.
How quickly life changes direction.

Why

You call me egoistic fool.
There's no point in turning my insides out anymore
to show I love you and to make you believe in me.

And here I am writing another poem
morning after an agonizing night
thinking about you.

Making a cup of tea
gazing out the kitchen window
exhausted
hoping that day will be better.

I have shown you
how I feel inside
but you ignored
as if you saw nothing.

I tell you how my soul bleeds
by your behavior.

I tell you how I pray for grace
and receive pain.

I tell you how I die
every time you look away
yet here I am
victim of my own actions.

I confess
I try hard not to judge anymore.
I don't pray anymore
unless undressing my soul
is a prayer.

Ashok K. Bhargava

The future is all there is. My gift
to myself is past memories.
Ephemeral yet they
still provide context
saving my life.

My Useless Words

Without you
I exist in the confines of a wall
I have built within myself.
Expecting it to last
Until the sun rises.

I exist
Like an abstract poem
Full of crazy metaphors
Outlandish
Rhymeless.

I know you are there
at the bend of the path.
I wait for you to appear.
Not knowing when
Maybe tomorrow or maybe never
Yet I keep waiting.

One day I might find you
Walking in
To undo the past
To bind us together
Again.

Ashok K. Bhargava

Caroline 'Ceri Naz' Nazareno Gabis

Caroline 'Ceri' Nazareno-Gabis

Caroline 'Ceri Naz' Nazareno-Gabis, author of Velvet Passions of Calibrated Quarks, World Poetry Canada International Director to Philippines is a multi-awarded poet, editor, journalist, educator, peace and women's advocate. She believes that learning other's language and culture is a doorway to wisdom.

Among her poetic belts include **Gabrielle Galloni Memorial Panorama International Youth Award** 2022, Panorama Youth Literary Awards 2020, 7th Prize Winner in the 19th, 20th and 21st Italian Award of Literary Festival; Writers International Network-Canada ''Amazing Poet 2015'', The Frang Bardhi Literary Prize 2014 (Albania), Poet Journalist Award 2014 (Tuzla, Istanbul, Turkey) and World Poetry Empowered Poet 2013 (Vancouver, Canada). She's a featured member of Association of Women's Rights and Development (AWID), The Poetry Posse, Galaktika Poetike, Asia Pacific Writers and Translators (APWT), Axlepino and Anacbanua. Her poetry and children's stories have been featured in different anthologies and magazines worldwide.

Links to her works:

http://panitikan.ph/2018/03/30/caroline-nazareno-gabis/

https://apwriters.org/author/ceri_naz/

http://www.aveviajera.org/nacionesunidasdelasletras/id1181.html

Caroline 'Ceri' Nazareno-Gabis

Forelsket

When the orchids bloom,

It dawns a world so calm,

A quiet spark that trembles inside,

It breathes a love divine and free,

The warmth of its fire glows and burns,

Moments rush like waves,

But the beating current and love hush

Let it sing and dance eternally!

Moledro

(deep connection to the artist's work)
Let me be a fleeting brush
A gentle, soft thread
That trace is like sweet pea's petals
Pressed in the pages,
Let me be the echoes of gratitude,
That capture your ears to listen well,
And will linger in your imagination,
A weightless touch that time will bear,
Let me be the gems engraved in your mind,
The ghost of grace that haunts you,
That hums in quiet air,
A promise left everlasting,
So let them rest where memories sleep,
where thankful spirits are called for keeps.

Pneuma
Breath of Life

Your presence is woven everywhere,

Unseen but felt,

The pulse of everything is in place,

Under the boundless sky,

Footprints may fade,

But the imprints you make,

Lifts a heart in a full circle,

A sacred air that comes in open doors,

The gift of contentment through the years,

A mortal's breath of life.

Swapna Behera

Swapna Behera

Swapna Behera is a trilingual poet, translator, environmentalist, editor from India and author of seven books of different genres including one on children's literature on Environment. She is the recipient of International UGADI AWARD 2019, honoured from Gujurat Sahitya Akademi 2022, 2021 International Poesis Award of Honor as Jury, Pentasi B World Fellow Poet, Honoured Poet of India from Seychelles Government and International awards from Algeria, Morocco, Kajhakhstan, modern Arabic Literary Renaissance of Egypt, International Arts Council Argentina etc. Her stories, poems, articles are published in many International and National magazines and ezines. Her poem A NIGHT IN THE REFUGEE CAMP is translated into 67 languages. She has received over 60 National and International Awards. At present she is the Cultural Ambassador for India and South Asia of Inner Child and the life member of Odisha Environmental Society

Email
swapna.behera@gmail.com

Web Site
http://swapnabehera.in/

I am in love - - -

love is in the air
love is in the moon
love is in the flowers
love is in water
because love is life

love is in the hemisphere
love is beyond the galaxy
love is at home
love is in the ether
because love is a star

love is in the ocean
love is in the clouds
love is in the Sun
love is in the forest
because love is the Nature

love is in the heart
love is in the body
love is in the soul
love is in the mind
because love wants to live

love is in the crowd
love is in the solitude
love is a woman
love is a man
because love needs love

love is in the hospital
love is in the graveyard
love is in the school
love is in the orphanage
because love is a soul

love is in the church
love is in the temple
love is in the mosque
Love is in the Gurudwara
Because love has no religion

love is mine
love is yours
love is theirs
Love is ours
because love is a feeling

love is a smile
love is in tears
love is a day
love is a night
because love is beyond time

love is a vision
love is a mission
love is a sacrifice
love is a fragrance
because love is mellifluous

you are in love
I am in love
the river is in love
the love is in love
because love is in the air - - - - -

Swapna Behera

aroma of beatitude

aroma of life
moments in Paradise

aroma of love
the layers of nimbus

aroma of sorrow
the domain of ego

aroma of words
the voyage of the dictum

aroma of emotions
the legitimate rainbows

aroma of fear
royal escorts of the track

aroma of lust
intent vicious passion

aroma of beatitude
perfumes of gratitude

aroma of light
may be melting self silently - - -

How I wish !!

How I wish
my prayers, my words
fly from me to nature
receive the energy of love and care

How I wish
my prayers fly
from one nation to the other
to sing and console the distressed
to delete the jealousies and envies
and all wrong memories

How I wish
to cheer up every soul that I meet
to be responsible
for the nature, for the globe,
for me for the humanity

Forgive me oh Lord
my impatience, my intolerance
forgive me for the things that I couldn't complete
give me the strength
to protect the nature and me
bless the little children
sick in the hospital
give me the fine impulses,
the vibes to live for others

Help me oh Lord
to explore my inner strength
to praise the beauty of others
to analyse my own self
to look into the need of others
to be grateful

How I wish ……..

Swapna Behera

Albert 'Infinite' Carrasco

Albert 'Infinite' Carassco

Albert "Infinite The Poet" Carrasco is an urban poet, mentor and public speaker.

Albert believes his experience of growing up in poverty, dealing with drugs and witnessing murder over and over were lessons learnt, in order to gain knowledge to teach. Albert's harsh reality and honesty is a powerfully packed punch delivered through rhyme. Infinite grew up in the east part of the Bronx and still resides there, so he knows many young men will follow the same dark path he followed looking for change. The life of crime should never be an option to being poor but it is, very often.

Infinite poetry @lulu.com

Alcarrasco2 on YouTube

Infinite the poet on reverbnation

Infinite Poetry

www.lulu.com/us/en/shop/al-infinite-carrasco/infinite-poetry/paperback/product-21040240.html

www.innerchildpress.com/albert-carrasco

Love, Gratitude, Contentment

Love is the highest form of understanding yourself as well as someone else, before we can love others we must learn to love thy self. If love was spread all over the world there wouldn't be any suicide or murders, we'll all have each other's back regardless if we're white, black or any color in between and live as brothers and sisters. There would be no borders, the only thing that should separate us is water, not language, religion nor colors. Imagine a life like that. There will be global gratitude, hate and war wouldn't exist, anywhere we travel respect will be shown at the highest magnitude no matter the meeting point of longitude and latitude. Joy and laughter will be contagious, the feeling of being welcomed without judgment would be infinitely continuous. Repetitive love would last forever if I keep loving you and you keep loving me and he keeps loving her and she keeps loving him etcetera etcetera. Unfortunately life isn't like that right now but that doesn't mean that we can't make it that way, I have hope and I pray that one day there will be universal contentment throughout every continent

Kimberly Burnham

Kimberly Burnham

A brain health expert (PhD in Integrative Medicine) and award-winning poet, Kimberly Burnham lives with her wife and family in Spokane, Washington. Kim speaks extensively on peace, brain health, and *"Awakenings: Peace Dictionary, Language and the Mind, a Daily Brain Health Program."* She recently published *"Heschel and King Marching to Montgomery A Jewish Guide to Judeo-Tamarian Imagery."* Currently work includes *"Call and Response To Maya Stein an Anthology of Wild Writing"* and a how-to non-fiction book, *"Using Ekphrastic Fiction Writing and Poetry to Create Interest and Promote Artists, Writers, and Poets."*

Follow her at https://amzn.to/4fcWnRB

Saving My World

"My heart is moved by all I cannot save" ... a line from
Adrienne Rich
I can vote but I can only know what is in my own interests
others, family, dear friends have their own view of how to
save the world

I cannot save a friend from the pain of divorce
any more than I could save myself from broken
relationships in the past
I can only look forward and do better in my own
relationship
I can learn from my own history

I cannot save the deer from the cold on a late fall day
a deer the color of my beloved rescue dog Wally
grazes in the field on fallen leaves and the last green of the
season

I cannot save the green leaves
falling in deep piles in patterns of yellow and red
concentric circles around the trees
overlapping creating interest

I cannot save the kitten on Nextdoor
in desperate need of a new home
without causing an uproar in the house
balancing the needs of our old cat and two rescue dogs

I cannot save all the papers that come in the door
magazines, flyers, paper from our printer
one day I might need this information I tell myself
but for the sake of my heart
I must let go of what I cannot save
so I can love what is still here in my world

Praise Song

Praise the bunnies running wild in the front garden
staying away from the dogs in the backyard
Praise the violinist and guitar player at the jazz concert
as the music carried me away from my stressors
Praise the Jewish community trying to do the right thing
struggling to find the way forward from war
Praise the rain falling this spring on the rhubarb, strawberries, onions
and the apple trees covered in white blossoms turning to red fruit
Praise the sunlight sparkling off the leaves wet from the overnight rain
greening up and nourishing the land
Praise the dandelions brightly sprinkled through the lawn
providing food for the bees and honey for my table
Praise the wind blowing in the trees bringing rain clouds
and change, new opportunities, and spinning metal art
Praise unconditional love and the broken path that led me here
to a place of peace and gratitude
Praise stepchildren, hope, and learning
and children everywhere planting and growing the future
Praise books and knowledge and ways to share
what bits I know about this world
Praise dogs, cuddly companions even on dark days
with a big warm body, wet tongue, and irrepressible curiosity
Praise art, this beauty manifested, copied, created,
a reflection of what is good in the world
Praise boxes and bags, containers for the stuff of life
I am not yet ready to let go, even seeing that I am holding too much

Kimberly Burnham

Praise drums, beating out the sound
of the rhythms in my hands and in the earth
Praise poetry giving an outlet to emotions, gratitude, and love
all with the space to create my world a new each morning

The First Day

"You tell me to live each day
as if it were my last. Why not
live each day as if it were the first—
all raw astonishment"
—Linda Pastan, Imaginary Conversation

Before I live each day as if it were my first
I have questions

Would I still know what I know
learning from my history trying to do better
failing sometimes but still living the best version of myself

Would I still be able to talk, communicate
know things I learned as a baby or teenager
when my parents in jest put on the fridge
"leave home while you still know everything"

Would I have stuff, a wardrobe of comfortable pants
and button up shirts to choose from on each first day
books to read, podcasts to listen to
a bicycle, the one I rode across the country
but now don't make time for as much

Would you be beside me
would I know that is where you have been for the past 12 years
my love and appreciation still growing each day
as I look at our wedding pictures

Would I know how to work as a manual therapist
and remember all the techniques, acupressure points,
names of muscles and bones, how the blood flows

and nerves communicate, telling us
about the newness in the world around us

Would I know how to write, styles of poetry,
how to share my heart, and what I love, or grammar rules
and different languages all remnants of my history on earth

Would I know how to drive, obey the rules of the road
where the kids school is or the grocery store
what time I have to leave the house to get them there on time

Would I have the seeds I bought last week to plant
sunflowers and squash
or the cans of cat food would I know he tries to trick me
into giving him three cans a day
rubbing himself on my leg and crying as if he is a starving stray
but we only give him two cans plus unlimited dry food

Would I see the pieces of foil on my desk
and know it is to prevent the cat from jumping up
knocking over my tea, would I know I prefer herbal tea
that I grew up Mormon and never developed a taste for coffee

Would I know how to keep the kitchen kosher
that the red edged utensils are for meat
and blue plates are for dairy
the glass can be used for either one

Would I know the password for my phone or computer
what games are my favorites
or what chapter I am working on in my latest book
would I get an email saying a long lost relative has died

and I just need to pay $200 for the mailing fee on the inheritance
would I know it is a scam

There are so many questions I have
before committing to living each day as my first
but I can easily commit to more astonishment, appreciation
and joy in the living of my life

Kimberly Burnham

Eliza Segiet

Eliza Segiet

Eliza Segiet graduated with a Master's Degree in Philosophy at Jagiellonian University.

Received *Global Literature Guardian Award* – from Motivational Strips, World Nations Writers Union and Union Hispanomundial De Escritores (UHE) 2018.

Nominated for the Pushcart Prize 2019, 2021.

Laureate *Naji Naaman Literary Prize 2020*,

International Award Paragon of Hope (2020),

World Award 2020 *Cesar Vallejo* for Literary Excellence. Laureate of the Special Jury *Sahitto International Award* 2021, World Award *Premiul Fănuș Neagu* 2021.

Finalist *Golden Aster Book* World Literary Prize 2020, *Mili Dueli* 2022, Voci nel deserto 2022.

At the international Festival of Poetry CAMPIONATO MONDIALE DI POESIA (2021/2022) she won the title of vice-champion of the world.

Award BHARAT RATNA RABINDRANATH TAGORE INTERNATIONAL AWARD (2022).

Award - *World Poets Association* (2023).

Laureate Between words and infinity *"International Literary Award (2023).*

Above All Else

Clairvoyant,
raven-black beauty
foretold the future,
reading it from the roar of the waves.
Standing on the bank,
she whispered to the bride-to-be:
– *Don't do it. He will…*
She stopped. She saw her tears,
the fear of a day with a double:
I will.

She sensed the woman's anxiety,
her fear for her unborn child
and the future
– without a future.
They both knew
that a ring on her finger would not make life easier,
and a child's peace of mind was the most important.
It's worth
to give oneself fully to someone
you have not seen yet,
but already loved above all else.

Translated by Dorota Stępińska

Diamond

When fate comes with a smile,

even

bad weather cannot hinder

the shining hope.

Between the possibilities of choice,

we find a diamond,

granting tomorrow

 – the brilliance of reality.

Bliss fuels existence,

melancholy takes away the meaning of dreams.

Translated by Dorota Stępińska

The Color of White

Snowdrops
showed their beauty –
this
magic possessed her mind.
The flowers heralded the end of winter.
The long, cold evenings
were to be fading into oblivion.
She didn't like this time of year –
she loved the sun,
it brought hope,
life and a colourful
joyful future.

Her
 – peace had the color of white,
 – the rising sun brought joy.
She loved embracing the summer,
it was her encouragement to
 – act,
 – create,
 – be happy.

Translated by Dorota Stępińska

William S. Peters Sr.

William S. Peters, Sr.

Bill's writing career spans a period of well over 50 years. Being first Published in 1972, Bill has since went on to Author in excess of 50+ additional Volumes of Poetry, Short Stories, etc., expressing his thoughts on matters of the Heart, Spirit, Consciousness and Humanity. His primary focus is that of Love, Peace and Understanding!

Bill says . . .

I have always likened Life to that of a Garden. So, for me, Life is simply about the Seeds we Sow and Nourish. All things we "Think and Do", will "Be" Cause and eventually manifest itself to being an "Effect" within our own personal "Existences" and "Experiences" . . . whether it be Fruit, Flowers, Weeds or Barren Landscapes! Bill highly regards the Fruits of his Labor and wishes that everyone would thus go on to plant "Lovely" Seeds on "Good Ground" in their own Gardens of Life!

to connect with Bill, he is all things Inner Child

www.iaminnerchild.com

Personal Web Site

www.iamjustbill.com

Love, Gratitude, Contentment

I reached out my hand
Seeking to touch
Love once again

I was and am ever thankful
To still be able
To do so

This is my contentment
To be able to try
To love

Love, Gratitude, Contentment

Unrequited

It was a
Supremely special serendipitous Sunday
When i first played my eyes
Upon her countenance ....
My God did she have an aura....
I could even see a
Light filled golden halo
Floating gracefully
About 8 inches
Above her head

Church, though I did not attend,
She instantaneously captured my attention,
And I nailed myself
To a proverbial cross
And begged for forgiveness
When I first laid my empty eyes
Upon her countenance....
I thus became
A wanton vagrant
Smitten by a need
I did not understand ...
I knew with a heart driven certainty
That i wanted to know her

The image of her
Became my salvation
For i learned
A new meaning of
Unrequited love.

Re-Fractal

Refractal reflections
Of a life gone by
And we humans oft ask
The question 'why'

Patch-quilt dreams
Of hopes to come
Neglectful we are
Of our holy sum

We Were created to conquer
Yet we oft times lie
In await for an end
Where we believe we die

We are strong and powerful
But we only suspect
Our Soul's potential
Awoken not yet

As time goes by
And its illusions embraced
Truth is a fear
Rarely by us faced

But somewhere deeply buried
In the soul of us all
Is a power and knowing
Awaiting our call

Nowhere is it written
That we were born to accept
This maleable fate
That is quite suspect

Let us gather ourselves people
And press ourselves forward
For this novel we now write
Is only the fore-word

Telling of content
Yet to unfold
When we fulfill the promises
Spoken of old

I believe soon come the day
When we open our eyes
And the truth of our divinity
Will be fully realized

Re-Fractal

William S. Peters, Sr.

June 2025 Featured Poets

Ayham Mahmoud Al-Abbad

Til Kumari Sharma

Michael Lee Johnson

Sylwia K. Malinowska

Ayham Mahmoud Al-Abbad

Ayham Mahmoud Al-Abbad

Ayham Mahmoud Al-Abbad is an Iraqi poet and academic, born in Al-Alam (1987). Ph.D in Translation. His poems were translated into English and published in the book (Voices from Iraq) in USA. Member of: Union of Writers in Iraq.

His poetic works:

- A Shy Dance, Baghdad 2015.
- Before the World Goes Extinct, Baghdad 2019.
- A Memorial Photo in Paradise, Basra 2021.
-His translated works:
- Articles and Lectures, Oscar Wilde, Baghdad 2021.
- Studies in Pessimism, Arthur Schopenhauer, Baghdad 2022.
-Discourse and the Production of Knowledge, Van Dijke, Damascus 2023.

Ayham Mahmoud Al-Abbad

A Mole on Your Right Cheek

Someday,
I'll wave to you from a distance
When you look at the end of the bridge
You will surely know me.
Because I came to you with one arm missed by war,
And with a lonely heart, but with many fingers it sculpts to pick up what fell from the baggage of poets,
And when you are looking forward, I assure you, when you are looking out from the Bridge of the Martyrs
I'll catch you with my lonely arm
I hide you in my left pocket
Like a missing page from an ancient pagan book.
Someday,
I will tell you about the depression caused by your absence
And about empty valium tapes
And the picture I drew for you
With long hair and two dimples
But it doesn't quite match your features
When I first saw you in Mansour.
Tonight,
I will promise you
Like a catholic covenant between two lovers
When my voice pulls you
To the climax of the dream
I run my fingers over the phone
And I will pick you up something from the slanderers.
This is how you go to sleep
But me,
I'll just take a valium pill
Then I contemplate the virtual our selfie that we captured together
On New Year's Eve.

A Rare Disease

Before I sat in front of the ear, nose and throat doctor, I used to recall all the Ayas I had memorized of patience for affliction.

The doctor said: you have strained your ears to hear the anthems, and this will cost you a lot of time and money in the treatment journey. I sighed for a long time before answering with a rare poetic awareness:

I can renounce four senses at once, but keep my hearing forever. I want to persevere in hearing my beloved when she says: "Good morning, my most beautiful poet".

Then all my five senses are complete.

Ayham Mahmoud Al-Abbad

The Last Scenario

A child playing with a matchbox.
So what ?
A guard at the gate of a city ruined by the plague.
And what ?
An obscure poet writes bad poems.
I count my losses in the first week:
Another rose died in the garden.
Emotional crisis in Gemini.
Rumor has it that I'm leaving with a heart attack.
…………
…………
No
Not your face
Which doesn't light up my life twice.
I will die immediately
And I crash
Like a paper letter in a mailbox.
…………
…………
I put my heart on the dream
And launched a telescope over Baghdad,
I want to accurately measure the beam of your face
As you read my poem,
And I gather from you countless
Of light
And fragments of words.
…………
…………
Stranger between four walls
Stranger inside myself
My room is completely empty of you,
completely devoid of me,
I am, without you, a lifeless being.
…………
…………

My flaws: a boat that is tormented by time
I asked you, like Omar Sharif to Faten Hamama:
"Reform the corruption of my heart, or love me with all this ruin".
…………..
…………..
I'll pick up my plank and walk
Like Christ,
And I draw my martyrdom
Good news of your return,
Oh my last supper.

Ayham Mahmoud Al-Abbad

Til Kumari Sharma

Til Kumari Sharma

Ms. Til Kumari Sharma is Multi Award Winner in writing from an international area is from Paiyun 7- Hile Parbat, Nepal. She is known as Pushpa Bashyal around her community. Her writings are published in many countries. She is featured-poet and best-selling co-author too. She is a poet of World Record Book "HYPERPOEM". She is one of many artists to break a participant record to write a poem about the Eiffel Tower of France. Her *World Personality* is published in *Multiart Magazine* from Argentina. She is a feminist poet. She is published as the face of continent (Cover Page of Asia) in _Humanity Magazine_ of Russia. Her writing had started from Kirtipur, Kathmandu, Nepal.

Til Kumari Sharma

Beauty of Nature

The extreme beauty in the universe is nature.
There is sublimity with spirituality.
The glory of life flourishes here.
Nature is the supreme mother of the heart,
Shining and dancing around the universe.
Nature is colorful and magnetic source.
She heals our wound and pain.
She nourishes the mind with positive scene.
Nature is the supreme beauty in the earth.
She is glorious beauty in her inner and outer source.
Her beauty motivates to make me artist.
Her beauty keeps me near her excellence.
Her inspiration is my source of living.
Her cuteness invites me near.
I am the nearest and the dearest lover of her.
Where spirituality flourishes there.
Her sober appearance glorifies my art.
Her pure and virgin body is appraisable everywhere.
That purity I write for her beauty.
Her loyalty is my inspiration to write.

Tomb of Earthly Eternity

The glorious tomb of mine was before my birth.
That was decorated with shining glory.
The tomb was like heaven to flower my art.
The green soul was planted to have frequent birth.
Tomb was little home to keep my privacy.
Love was lost and kidnapped before my birth.
That I took the words to furnish my lively birth.
My tomb was really different than others.
The another birth appears with hard struggle as I felt in the grave.
After birth, I see no true people around me.
The life of the people spends with every faults and money.
Like hell, the people are living
With materialistic joy and showy beauty.
Wisdom is chaos in this earth.
Fashion is the foremost physical joy.
I see better my former tomb.
I see that the art flourishes there highly.
Tomb is not finishing life.
It gives memory of past life.
Still I love my tomb which does not make life as ashes of desert.
But flourishes there the art of eternity.

Wounded Love in the Battlefield and Hierarchy

Love in reality blooms the life.
When success appears.
When separation, wound takes place.
The love of conflicts is like hell of death.
There is not any love when mind and heart are not one.
Love is sick when deception arrives.
Love is breathless when lover exchanges many partners.
Wounded love is poison to kill.
No weapon is needed to loss life.
Silent enemy is deceptive love.
That is not possible to turn again in the same battlefield to get separated love.
Then beauty with eternity enters in the art of tears.
When deception appears with hate and negativity, true love disappears.
Hierarchy and caste bring the conflicts in love.
City and village are becoming battlefield of conflicted love.
To endure deception is great light to art.
Wounded battlefield is no need in love.
But true love is impossible in this materialistic and money loving earth.

Michael Lee Johnson

Michael Lee Johnson

Michael Lee Johnson is a poet of high acclaim, with his work published in 46 countries or republics. He is also a song lyricist with several published poetry books. His talent has been recognized with 7 Pushcart Prize nominations and 6 Best of the Net nominations. He has over 653 published poems. His 330-plus YouTube poetry videos are a testament to his skill and dedication. He is a proud member of the Illinois State Poetry Society: http://www.illinoispoets.org/. His poems have been translated into several foreign languages. Awards/Contests: International Award of Excellence "Citta' Del Galateo-Antonio De Ferrariis" XI Edition 2024 Milan, Italy-Poetry. Poem, Michael Lee Johnson, *"If I Were Young Again."* Remember to consider me for Best of the Net or Pushcart nomination!

Michael Lee Johnson

I Feel Lightning in Your Wind

I feel light in a thunderstorm.
I electrify your touch through my veins.
I'm the greenery around your life
that breathes your earth into your lungs.
I challenge all your false decisions and doctrines
with the glory of my godliness.
I'm your syntax, your stoic,
your ears, your prize.
I walk daylight into your morning breath
allow you to breathe.
I let the technique of me into your brain cells;
from the top tip to the bottom
of small baby foot extensions.
I'm the banquet hall of all
your joys, damnation;
your curses, your emotions—
and you're breathing with the wind.

April Winds

April winds persist
in doing charity work
early elbowing right to left
their way through these willow trees
branches melting reminiscences
of winter remnants off my condo roof
no snow crystals sprinkle
in drops over my balcony deck.
Canadian geese wait impatiently for their
spring feeding on the oozy ground below.
These silent sounds
except for the roar of laughter
those April winds—
geese hear nothing
no droppings from the balcony—
no seeds.

Michael Lee Johnson

Down by the Bridge

I'm the magic moment on magic mushrooms
$10 a gram, amphetamines, heroin for less.
Homeless, happy, Walmart discarded pillow
found in a puddle with a reflection,
down and dirty in the rain—down by the bridge.
Old street-time lover, I found the old bone man we share.
I'm in my butt-stink underwear, bra torn apart,
pants worn out, and holes in all the wrong places.
In the Chicago River, a free washing machine.
Flipped out on Lucifer's nighttime journey,
Night Train Express, bum wine, smooth
as sandpaper, 17.5 % alcohol by volume $5.56—
my boozer, hobo specialty wrapped in a brown bag.
Straight down the hatch, negative memories expire.
Daytime job, panhandling, shoplifting, Family Dollar store.
Salvation Army as an option. My prayers. I've done both.
Chicago River sounds, stone, pebble sand,
and small dead carp float by.
My cardboard bed box is broken down,
a mattress of angel fluff,
magic mushrooms seep into my stupor—
blocking out clicking of street parking meters.
I see Jesus passing by on a pontoon boat—
down by the river, down by my bridge.

Sylwia K. Malinowska

Sylwia K. Malinowska

Poet, occupational therapist, activist for the legalization of psychoactive plants and mushrooms. Through her work she calls for the freedom to decide for oneself about one's body and mind. She writes about love and respect for oneself, people and the world. Her texts have appeared in press publications such as "Poetry Today" and numerous books published in Polish, English, Bulgarian and Turkish. She is, among others, the author of the texts for the photo album by Beata Cierzniewska entitled "Cognition", presented in The Cooper House Gallery in Dublin. Her poems have also been presented in a joint project WAKE UP painting & poetry night at In-spire Gallery in Dublin. Recently her words have been published in her latest project in the book entitled: "The Power of Truth,about the difficult art of being yourself".

Sywia strives to inspire and heal with words, delving into herself and the mysterious world of nature, bringing out the beauty in humans and connecting with the uniqueness of nature , the thinking and feeling organism, Gaia.

Exist

When you awaken the force in you.
When you realize that there is a great force in you, that beauty is you.
The strength is you.
Sensitivity is you.
Truth.
Force.
It's you.
When you feel you're all you've been looking for, you're full, the source of everything.
When you touch the corners of your existence.
When you dive into yourself and don't look away.
When you swim somewhere on the verge of non-existence.
To places that aren't there, but are inside you.
When fear takes over your being,
that you stop being in it, stop existing, understanding what it is to be.
When you wander in infinity.
When you cross all boundaries.
When you understand that there is no turning back.
When you give up.
Simply fall.
Cease to exist.
When you feel a real touch of yourself that hurts because being who you are hurts you.
Then you will really feel, touch, and experience your beauty.

That spark.
Force.
Strength.
This unimaginable miracle.
Beauty.
Yes, that beauty.
Your existence.

Yourself

When you dare to touch yourself at least for a moment,
with a small fingertip and not to
look away.
Even though fear will crush every nook and cranny of your
mind and the truth will hurt.
When you feel that there is no other way, that there is no
turning back as you swim
towards trust, towards light, even though you do not know
what awaits you and fear
takes away your speech.
When you risk your whole life and stand behind you.
When you manage to take at least one tiny step, one!
Then......
You will see the truth about yourself.
And you will feel your beauty
Strength
And power.
And only then can we give another person a chance to see
the real us.
To get to know us, to touch us, to experience us.
Because only then do we have a chance to experience the
feeling of a deeper bond.
Because only then will the other person have a chance to
see not only the façade of
ourselves.
Because only then will we give them a chance to really get
closer to us

Sylwia K. Malinowska

Beautiful

Beauty is a power flowing from the knowledge of our nature. The brightness of the heart, the
light melting in the distance. Empathy and sensitivity in looking at other beings. It is a
conscious value and intention that comes from the heart in action. This is following the voice
of the heart when the whole world screams...no.

It is the forgiveness that gives solace and acceptance that brings peace.
Love, someone makes us great and the power that allows us to go on.
This certainty pushes you in one direction although the common sense pulls you by the
neck.
And although we do not know the future, we do not know what will happen next and we do
not know why we are here, we know that it is our identity, the individual color that defines us
in everyday life, separating the light line from the million others.
This power of striving for harmony and not perfection is beautiful

Remembering

our fallen soldiers of verse

Janet Perkins Caldwell
February 14, 1959 ~ September 20, 2016

Alan W. Jankowski
16 March 1961 ~ 10 March 2017

Shareef Abdur Rasheed
30 May 1945 ~ 11 February 2025

The Butterfly Effect

"IS" in effect

Inner Child Press

News

Published Books
by
Poetry Posse Members

We are so excited to share and announce a few of the current books, as well as the new and upcoming books of some of our Poetry Posse authors.

On the following pages we present to you ...

Alicja Maria Kuberska

Jackie Davis Allen

Gail Weston Shazor

hülya n. yılmaz

Nizar Sartawi

Elizabeth E. Castillo

Faleeha Hassan

Fahredin Shehu

Kimberly Burnham

Caroline 'Ceri' Nazareno

Eliza Segiet

Teresa E. Gallion

Mutawaf Shaheed

William S. Peters, Sr.

Now Available
www.innerchildpress.com

The Year of the Poet XII ~ June 2025

KREW ŻYCIA

The Blood of Life

Eliza Segiet

Translated by Dorota Stępińska

Now Available
www.innerchildpress.com

Inner Child Press News

Now Available
www.innerchildpress.com

The Year of the Poet XII ~ June 2025

Now Available
www.innerchildpress.com

Now Available
www.innerchildpress.com

The Year of the Poet XII ~ June 2025

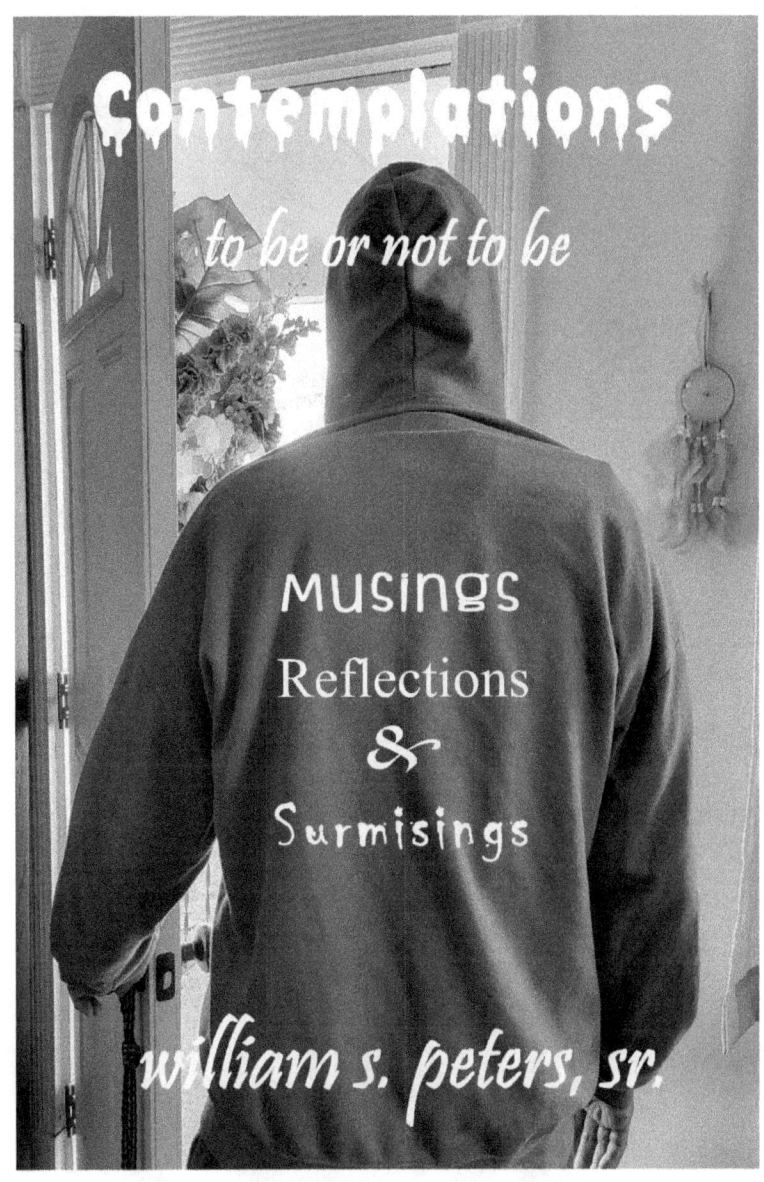

Now Available
www.innerchildpress.com

Inner Child Press News

Now Available
www.innerchildpress.com

The Year of the Poet XII ~ June 2025

Inner Child Press News

Now Available
www.innerchildpress.com

The Year of the Poet XII ~ June 2025

Now Available
www.innerchildpress.com

Inner Child Press News

Now Available
www.innerchildpress.com

The Year of the Poet XII ~ June 2025

Now Available
www.innerchildpress.com

Inner Child Press News

Now Available
www.innerchildpress.com

The Year of the Poet XII ~ June 2025

Now Available
www.innerchildpress.com

Inner Child Press News

Now Available at
www.innerchildpress.com

The Year of the Poet XII ~ June 2025

Now Available at
www.amazon.com/gp/product/B08MYL5B7S/ref=dbs_a_def_rwt_hsch_vapi_tkin_p1_i2

Inner Child Press News

Now Available
www.innerchildpress.com

The Year of the Poet XII ~ June 2025

Now Available
www.innerchildpress.com

Inner Child Press News

Now Available
www.innerchildpress.com

The Year of the Poet XII ~ June 2025

Now Available
www.innerchildpress.com

Inner Child Press News

Now Available
www.innerchildpress.com

The Year of the Poet XII ~ June 2025

Now Available
www.innerchildpress.com

Inner Child Press News

Now Available
www.innerchildpress.com

The Year of the Poet XII ~ June 2025

Now Available
www.innerchildpress.com

Inner Child Press News

Velvet Passions
of
Calibrated Quarks

Caroline Nazareno-Gabis

Now Available
www.innerchildpress.com

The Year of the Poet XII ~ June 2025

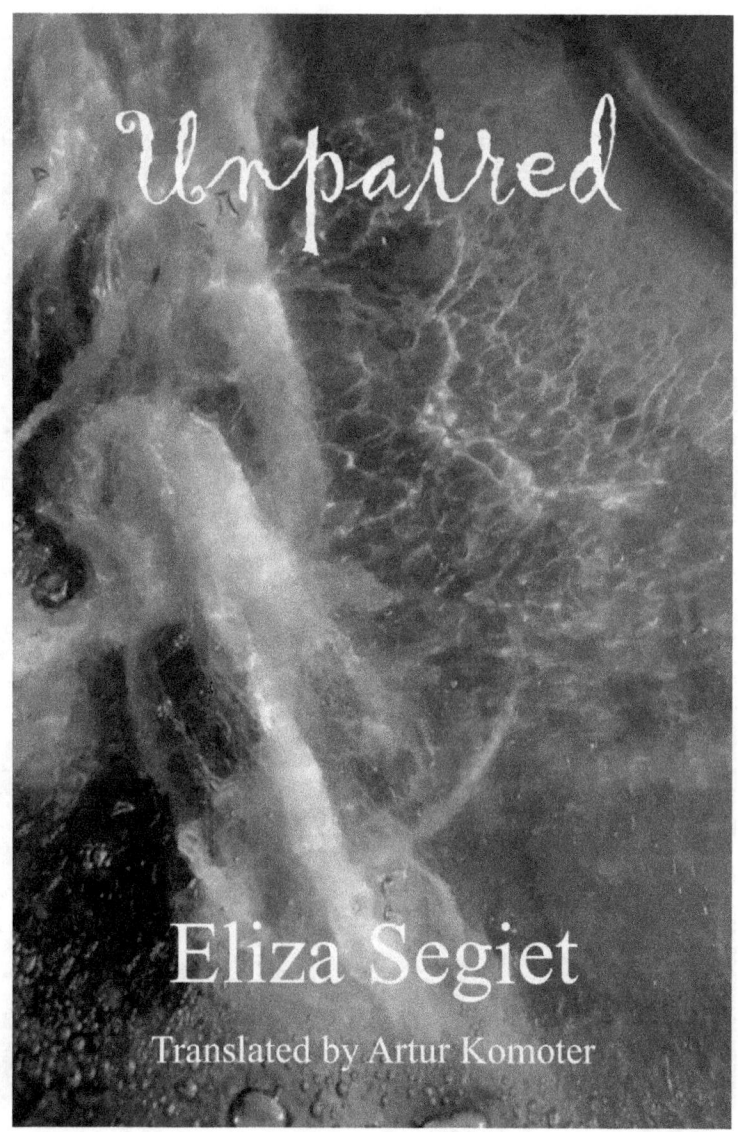

Now Available
www.innerchildpress.com

Private Issue
www.innerchildpress.com

The Year of the Poet XII ~ June 2025

Now Available at
www.innerchildpress.com

Now Available at
www.innerchildpress.com

The Year of the Poet XII ~ June 2025

Now Available at
www.innerchildpress.com

Now Available at
www.innerchildpress.com

The Year of the Poet XII ~ June 2025

HERENOW

FAHREDIN SHEHU

Now Available at
www.innerchildpress.com

Inner Child Press News

Now Available at
www.innerchildpress.com

The Year of the Poet XII ~ June 2025

Now Available at
www.innerchildpress.com

Inner Child Press News

Now Available at
www.innerchildpress.com

The Year of the Poet XII ~ June 2025

Now Available at
www.innerchildpress.com

Inner Child Press News

Now Available at
www.innerchildpress.com

The Year of the Poet XII ~ June 2025

Now Available at
www.innerchildpress.com

Inner Child Press News

Now Available at
www.innerchildpress.com

The Year of the Poet XII ~ June 2025

Now Available at
www.innerchildpress.com

Inner Child Press News

Now Available at
www.innerchildpress.com

The Year of the Poet XII ~ June 2025

Now Available at
www.innerchildpress.com

Inner Child Press News

Now Available
www.innerchildpress.com

Other Anthological works from

Inner Child Press International

www.innerchildpress.com

Inner Child Press Anthologies

Shareef
a soldier for
Allah

Patriarch, Activist & Humanitarian

Friends of the Pen

Now Available
www.innerchildpress.com/anthologies

Inner Child Press Anthologies

Now Available
www.innerchildpress.com

Inner Child Press Anthologies

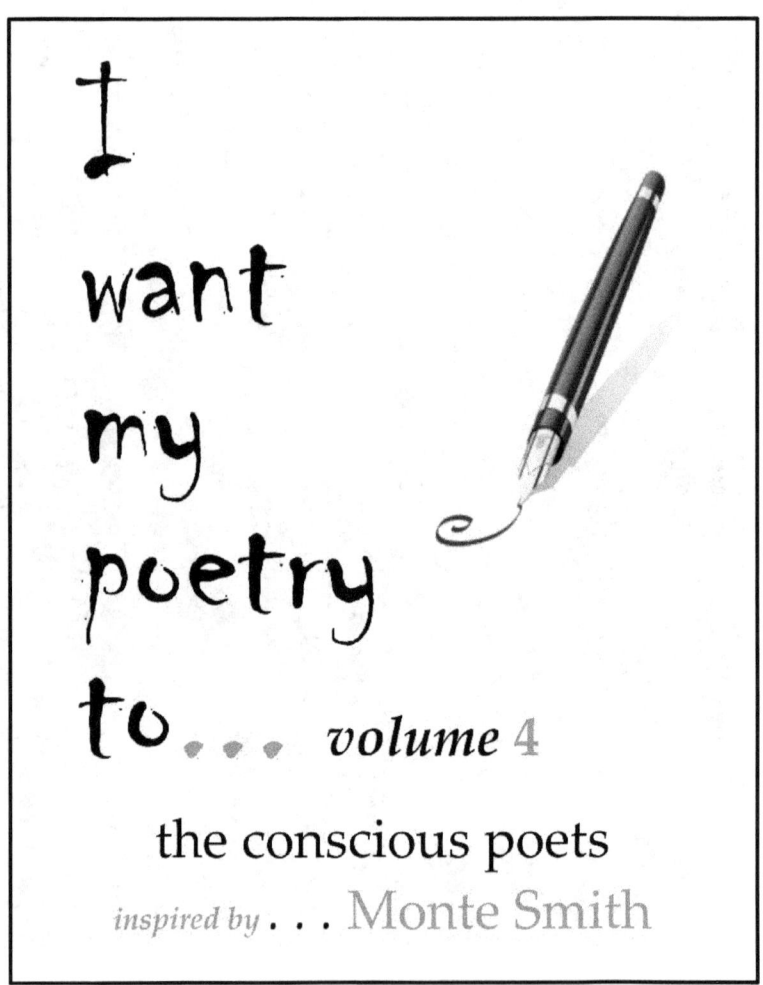

the conscious poets
inspired by . . . Monte Smith

Now Available
www.innerchildpress.com/anthologies

Inner Child Press Anthologies

Now Available
www.innerchildpress.com/anthologies

Inner Child Press Anthologies

Now Available
www.worldhealingworldpeacepoetry.com

Inner Child Press Anthologies

Now Available
www.innerchildpress.com/anthologies

Inner Child Press Anthologies

Now Available
www.worldhealingworldpeacepoetry.com

Inner Child Press Anthologies

Now Available
www.innerchildpress.com/anthologies

Inner Child Press Anthologies

Inner Child Press International
&
The Year of the Poet
present

Poetry
the best of 2020

Poets of the World

Now Available
www.innerchildpress.com/anthologies

Inner Child Press Anthologies

Now Available
www.innerchildpress.com/anthologies

Inner Child Press Anthologies

Now Available
www.innerchildpress.com/anthologies

Inner Child Press Anthologies

Now Available
www.innerchildpress.com/anthologies

Inner Child Press Anthologies

Now Available
www.innerchildpress.com/anthologies

Inner Child Press Anthologies

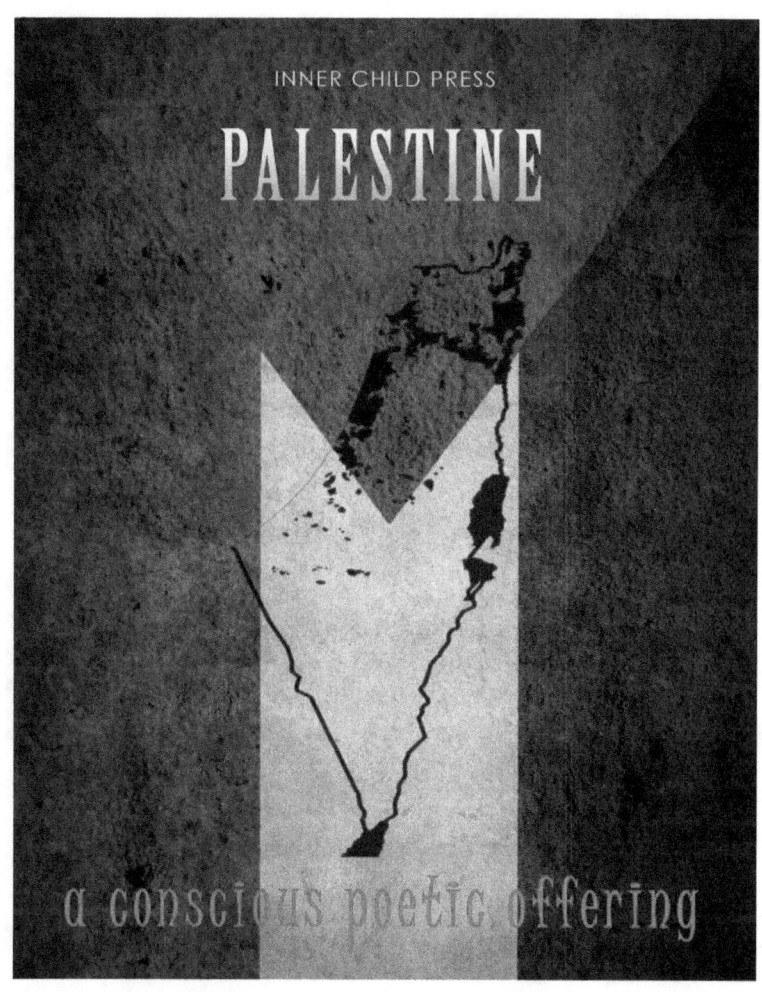

Now Available
www.innerchildpress.com/anthologies

Inner Child Press Anthologies

Now Available
www.innerchildpress.com/anthologies

Inner Child Press Anthologies

Now Available
www.innerchildpress.com/anthologies

Inner Child Press Anthologies

Now Available
www.worldhealingworldpeacepoetry.com

Inner Child Press Anthologies

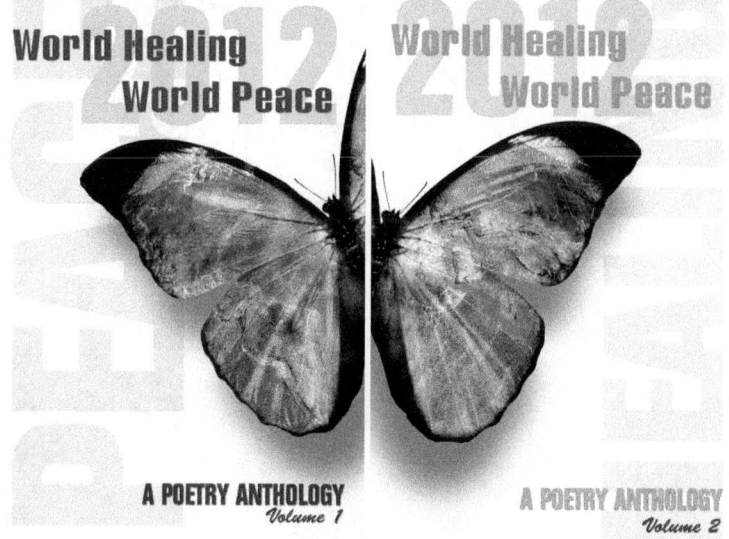

Now Available
www.worldhealingworldpeacepoetry.com

Inner Child Press Anthologies

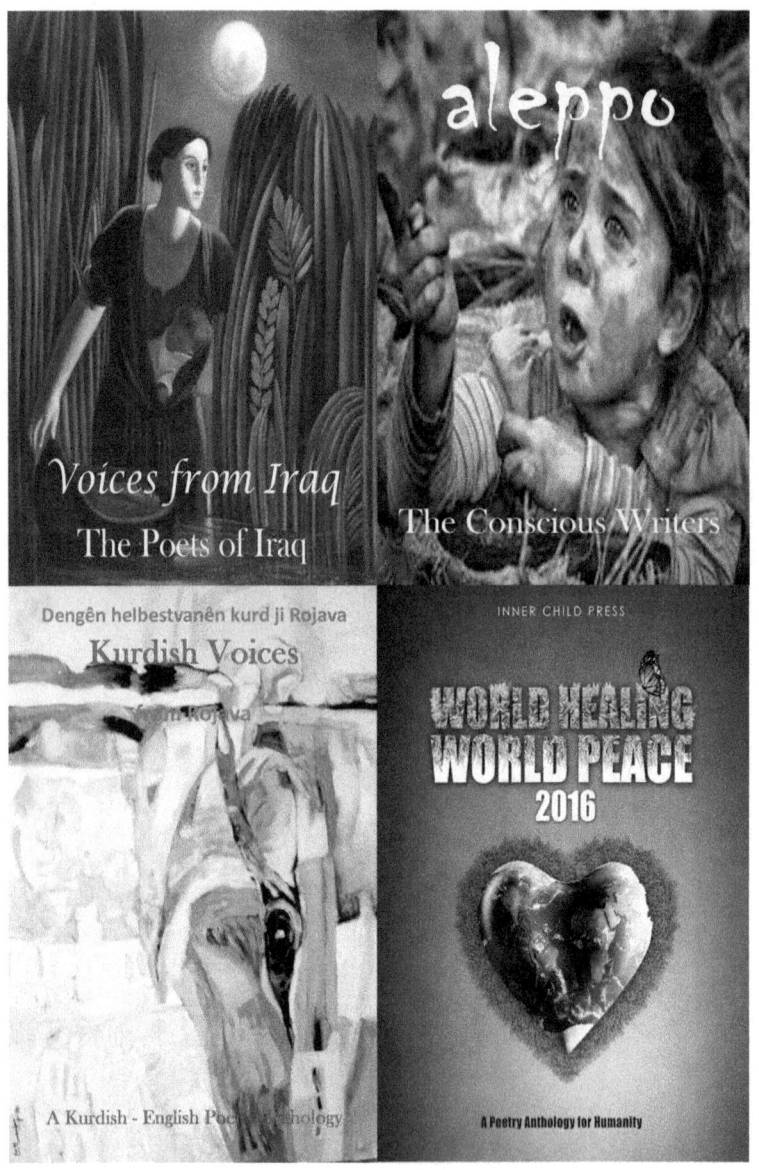

Now Available
www.innerchildpress.com/anthologies

Inner Child Press Anthologies

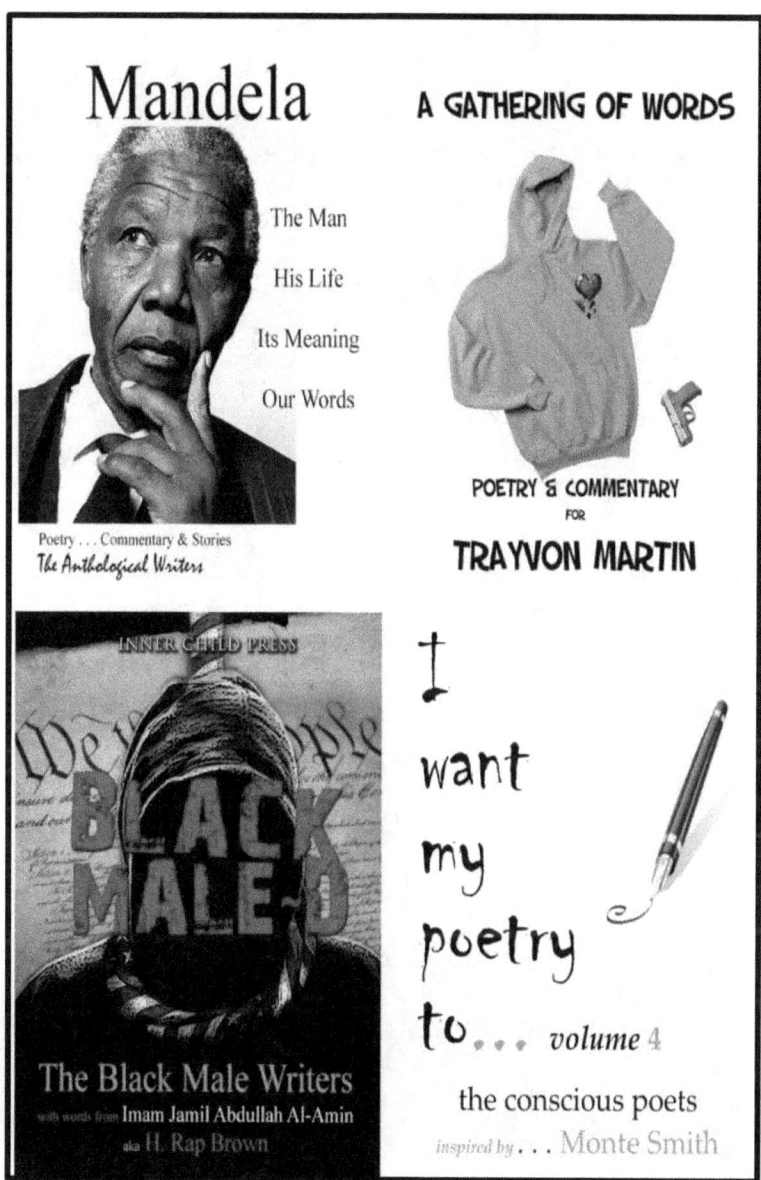

Now Available

www.innerchildpress.com/anthologies

Inner Child Press Anthologies

Now Available
www.innerchildpress.com/anthologies

Inner Child Press Anthologies

Now Available
www.innerchildpress.com/anthologies

Inner Child Press Anthologies

Now Available
www.innerchildpress.com/anthologies

Inner Child Press Anthologies

Now Available
www.innerchildpress.com/the-year-of-the-poet

Inner Child Press Anthologies

Now Available
www.innerchildpress.com/the-year-of-the-poet

Inner Child Press Anthologies

Now Available
www.innerchildpress.com/the-year-of-the-poet

Inner Child Press Anthologies

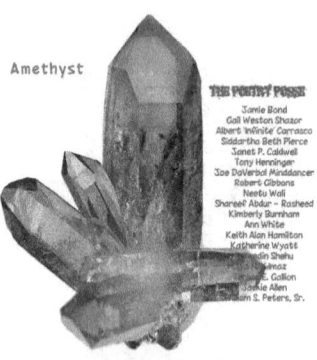

Now Available
www.innerchildpress.com/the-year-of-the-poet

Inner Child Press Anthologies

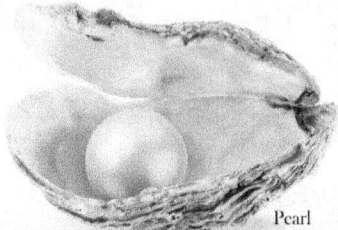

Now Available

www.innerchildpress.com/the-year-of-the-poet

Inner Child Press Anthologies

Now Available
www.innerchildpress.com/the-year-of-the-poet

Inner Child Press Anthologies

Now Available
www.innerchildpress.com/the-year-of-the-poet

Inner Child Press Anthologies

Now Available
www.innerchildpress.com/the-year-of-the-poet

Inner Child Press Anthologies

Now Available
www.innerchildpress.com/the-year-of-the-poet

Inner Child Press Anthologies

Now Available

www.innerchildpress.com/the-year-of-the-poet

Inner Child Press Anthologies

Now Available
www.innerchildpress.com/the-year-of-the-poet

Inner Child Press Anthologies

The Year of the Poet IV
September 2017

Featured Poets
Martina Reisz Newberry
Ameer Nassir
Christine Fulco Neal
Robert Neal

The Elm Tree

The Poetry Posse 2017

Gail Weston Shazor * Caroline Nazareno * Bismay Mohanty
Teresa E. Gallion * Anna Jakubczak Vel Ratty Adalan
Joe DaVerbal Minddancer * Shareef Abdur – Rasheed
Albert Carrasco * Kimberly Burnham * Elizabeth Castillo
Hülya N. Yılmaz * Faleeha Hassan * Jackie Davis Allen
Jen Walls * Nizar Sartawi * * William S. Peters, Sr.

The Year of the Poet IV
October 2017

Featured Poets
Ahmed Abu Saleem
Nedal Al-Qaeim
Sadeddin Shahin

The Black Walnut Tree

The Poetry Posse 2017

Gail Weston Shazor * Caroline Nazareno * Bismay Mohanty
Teresa E. Gallion * Anna Jakubczak Vel Ratty Adalan
Joe DaVerbal Minddancer * Shareef Abdur – Rasheed
Albert Carrasco * Kimberly Burnham * Elizabeth Castillo
Hülya N. Yılmaz * Faleeha Hassan * Jackie Davis Allen
Jen Walls * Nizar Sartawi * * William S. Peters, Sr.

The Year of the Poet IV
November 2017

Featured Poets
Kay Peters
Alfreda D. Ghee
Gabriella Garofalo
Rosemary Cappello

The Tree of Life

The Poetry Posse 2017

Gail Weston Shazor * Caroline Nazareno * Bismay Mohanty
Teresa E. Gallion * Anna Jakubczak Vel Ratty Adalan
Joe DaVerbal Minddancer * Shareef Abdur – Rasheed
Albert Carrasco * Kimberly Burnham * Elizabeth Castillo
Hülya N. Yılmaz * Faleeha Hassan * Jackie Davis Allen
Jen Walls * Nizar Sartawi * William S. Peters, Sr.

The Year of the Poet IV
December 2017

Featured Poets
Justice Clarke
Mariel M. Pabroa
Kiley Brown

The Fig Tree

The Poetry Posse 2017

Gail Weston Shazor * Caroline Nazareno * Bismay Mohanty
Teresa E. Gallion * Anna Jakubczak Vel Ratty Adalan
Joe DaVerbal Minddancer * Shareef Abdur – Rasheed
Albert Carrasco * Kimberly Burnham * Elizabeth Castillo
Hülya N. Yılmaz * Faleeha Hassan * Jackie Davis Allen
Jen Walls * Nizar Sartawi * William S. Peters, Sr.

Now Available

www.innerchildpress.com/the-year-of-the-poet

Inner Child Press Anthologies

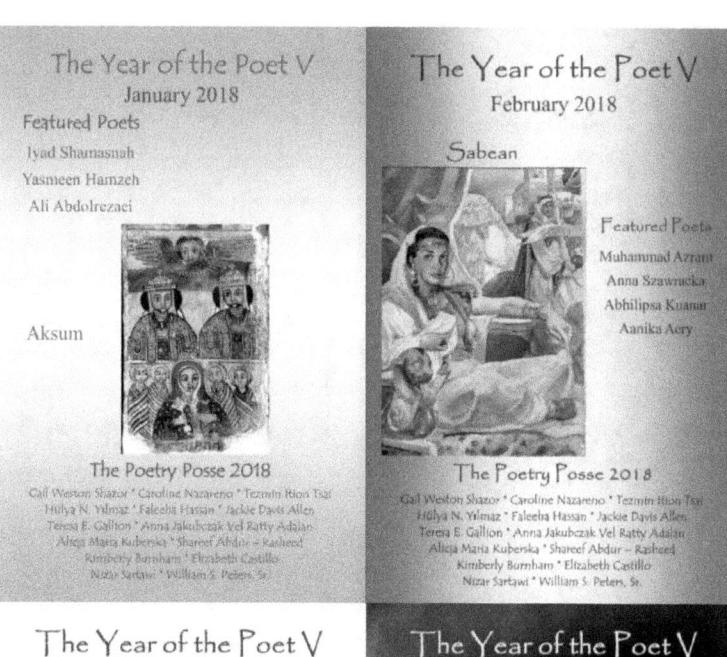

Now Available
www.innerchildpress.com/the-year-of-the-poet

Inner Child Press Anthologies

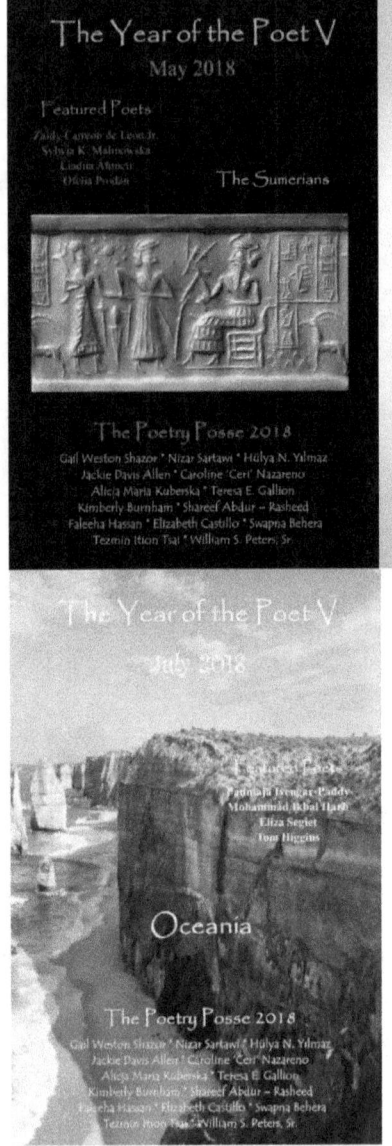

Now Available
www.innerchildpress.com/the-year-of-the-poet

Inner Child Press Anthologies

Now Available
www.innerchildpress.com/the-year-of-the-poet

Inner Child Press Anthologies

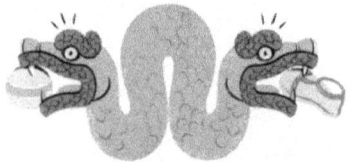

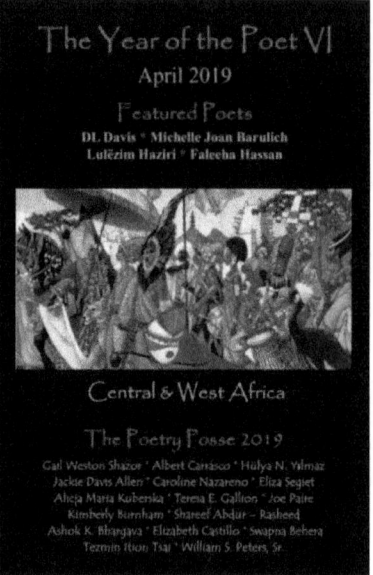

Now Available

www.innerchildpress.com/the-year-of-the-poet

Inner Child Press Anthologies

Now Available
www.innerchildpress.com/the-year-of-the-poet

Inner Child Press Anthologies

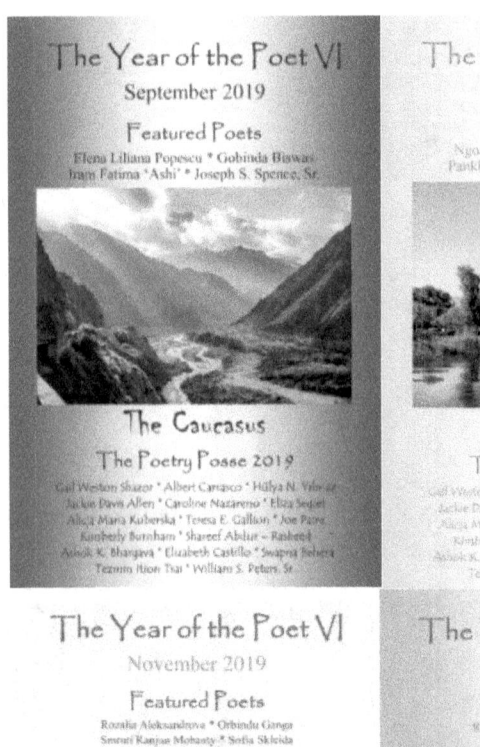

Now Available
www.innerchildpress.com/the-year-of-the-poet

Inner Child Press Anthologies

Now Available
www.innerchildpress.com/the-year-of-the-poet

Now Available

www.innerchildpress.com/the-year-of-the-poet

Inner Child Press Anthologies

Now Available
www.innerchildpress.com/the-year-of-the-poet

Inner Child Press Anthologies

The Year of the Poet VIII
January 2021

Featured Global Poets
Andrew Scott * Debaprasanna Biswas
Shakil Kalam * Changming Yuan

Banksy's The Girl with the Pierced Eardrum

Poetry ... Ekphrasticly Speaking
The Poetry Posse 2020

Gail Weston Shazor * Albert Carasco * Hülya N. Yılmaz
Jackie Davis Allen * Caroline Nazareno * Eliza Segiet
Alicja Maria Kuberska * Teresa E. Gallion * Joe Paire
Kimberly Burnham * Shareef Abdur – Rasheed
Ashok K. Bhargava * Elizabeth Castillo * Swapna Behera
Tezmin Ition Tsai * William S. Peters, Sr.

The Year of the Poet VIII
February 2021

Featured Global Poets
T. Ramesh Babu * Ruchida Barman
Neptune Barman * Faleeha Hassan

Emory Douglas : 1968 Olympics mural

Poetry ... Ekphrasticly Speaking
The Poetry Posse 2021

Gail Weston Shazor * Albert Carasco * Hülya N. Yılmaz
Jackie Davis Allen * Caroline Nazareno * Eliza Segiet
Alicja Maria Kuberska * Teresa E. Gallion * Joe Paire
Kimberly Burnham * Shareef Abdur – Rasheed
Ashok K. Bhargava * Elizabeth Castillo * Swapna Behera
Tezmin Ition Tsai * William S. Peters, Sr.

The Year of the Poet VIII
March 2021

Featured Global Poets
Claudia Piccinno * Mohammed Jabr
Luzviminda Rivera * Nigar Arif

Tatyana Fazlalizadeh

Poetry ... Ekphrasticly Speaking
The Poetry Posse 2021

Gail Weston Shazor * Albert Carasco * Hülya N. Yılmaz
Jackie Davis Allen * Caroline Nazareno * Eliza Segiet
Alicja Maria Kuberska * Teresa E. Gallion * Joe Paire
Kimberly Burnham * Shareef Abdur – Rasheed
Ashok K. Bhargava * Elizabeth Castillo * Swapna Behera
Tezmin Ition Tsai * William S. Peters, Sr.

The Year of the Poet VIII
April 2021

Featured Global Poets
Katarzyna Brus- Sawczuk * Anwesha Paul
Rozalia Aleksandrova * Shahid Abbas

Pablo O'Higgins

Poetry ... Ekphrasticly Speaking
The Poetry Posse 2021

Gail Weston Shazor * Albert Carasco * Hülya N. Yılmaz
Jackie Davis Allen * Caroline Nazareno * Eliza Segiet
Alicja Maria Kuberska * Teresa E. Gallion * Joe Paire
Kimberly Burnham * Shareef Abdur – Rasheed
Ashok K. Bhargava * Elizabeth Castillo * Swapna Behera
Tezmin Ition Tsai * William S. Peters, Sr.

Now Available
www.innerchildpress.com/the-year-of-the-poet

Inner Child Press Anthologies

Now Available
www.innerchildpress.com/the-year-of-the-poet

Inner Child Press Anthologies

The Year of the Poet VIII
September 2021

Featured Global Poets
Monsif Beroual * Sandesh Ghimire
Sharmila Poudel * Pavol Janik

Heather Jansch

Poetry ... Ekphrasticly Speaking

The Poetry Posse 2021
Gail Weston Shazor * Albert Carasco * Hülya N. Yılmaz
Jackie Davis Allen * Caroline Nazareno * Eliza Segiet
Alicja Maria Kuberska * Teresa E. Gallion * Joe Paire
Kimberly Burnham * Shareef Abdur – Rasheed
Ashok K. Bhargava * Elizabeth Castillo * Swapna Behera
Tezmin Ition Tsai * William S. Peters, Sr.

The Year of the Poet VIII
October 2021

Featured Global Poets
C. E. Shy * Saswata Ganguly
Suranjit Gain * Hasiba Hilal

Dale Lamphere

Poetry ... Ekphrasticly Speaking

The Poetry Posse 2021
Gail Weston Shazor * Albert Carasco * Hülya N. Yılmaz
Jackie Davis Allen * Caroline Nazareno * Eliza Segiet
Alicja Maria Kuberska * Teresa E. Gallion * Joe Paire
Kimberly Burnham * Shareef Abdur – Rasheed
Ashok K. Bhargava * Elizabeth Castillo * Swapna Behera
Tezmin Ition Tsai * William S. Peters, Sr.

The Year of the Poet VIII
November 2021

Featured Global Poets
Errol D. Bean * Ibrahim Honjo
Tanja Ajtic * Rajashree Mohapatra

Andy Goldsworthy

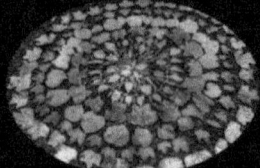

Poetry ... Ekphrasticly Speaking

The Poetry Posse 2021
Gail Weston Shazor * Albert Carasco * Hülya N. Yılmaz
Jackie Davis Allen * Caroline Nazareno * Eliza Segiet
Alicja Maria Kuberska * Teresa E. Gallion * Joe Paire
Kimberly Burnham * Shareef Abdur – Rasheed
Ashok K. Bhargava * Elizabeth Castillo * Swapna Behera
Tezmin Ition Tsai * William S. Peters, Sr.

The Year of the Poet VIII
December 2021

Featured Global Poets
Orbinda Ganga * Fadairo Tesleem
Anthony Arnold * Iyad Shamasnah

Fredric Edwin Church

Poetry ... Ekphrasticly Speaking

The Poetry Posse 2021
Gail Weston Shazor * Albert Carasco * Hülya N. Yılmaz
Jackie Davis Allen * Caroline Nazareno * Eliza Segiet
Alicja Maria Kuberska * Teresa E. Gallion * Joe Paire
Kimberly Burnham * Shareef Abdur – Rasheed
Ashok K. Bhargava * Elizabeth Castillo * Swapna Behera
Tezmin Ition Tsai * William S. Peters, Sr.

Now Available
www.innerchildpress.com/the-year-of-the-poet

Inner Child Press Anthologies

The Year of the Poet IX
January 2022

Featured Global Poets
**Ratan Ghosh * Christine Neil-Wright
Andrew Scott * Ashok Kumar**

Climate Change : The Ice Cap

Poetry . . . Ekphrasticly Speaking

The Poetry Posse 2021

Gail Weston Shazor * Albert Carasco * Hülya N. Yılmaz
Jackie Davis Allen * Caroline Nazareno * Eliza Segiet
Alicja Maria Kuberska * Teresa E. Gallion * Joe Paire
Kimberly Burnham * Shareef Abdur – Rasheed
Ashok K. Bhargava * Elizabeth Castillo * Swapna Behera
Tezmin Ition Tsai * William S. Peters, Sr.

The Year of the Poet IX
February 2022

Featured Global Poets
Roza Boyanova * Ramón de Jesús Núñez Duval
Mammad Ismayil * Tarana Turan Rahimli

Climate Change and Mountains

Poetry . . . Ekphrasticly Speaking

The Poetry Posse 2021

Gail Weston Shazor * Albert Carasco * Hülya N. Yılmaz
Jackie Davis Allen * Caroline Nazareno * Eliza Segiet
Alicja Maria Kuberska * Teresa E. Gallion * Joe Paire
Kimberly Burnham * Shareef Abdur – Rasheed
Ashok K. Bhargava * Elizabeth Castillo * Swapna Behera
Tezmin Ition Tsai * William S. Peters, Sr.

The Year of the Poet IX
March 2022

Featured Global Poets
Dimitris P. Kraniotis * Marlene Pasini
Kennedy Ochieng * Swayam Prashant

Climate Change and Space Debris

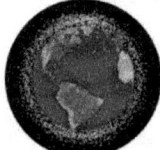

Poetry . . . Ekphrasticly Speaking

The Poetry Posse 2021

Gail Weston Shazor * Albert Carasco * Hülya N. Yılmaz
Jackie Davis Allen * Caroline Nazareno * Eliza Segiet
Alicja Maria Kuberska * Teresa E. Gallion * Joe Paire
Kimberly Burnham * Shareef Abdur – Rasheed
Ashok K. Bhargava * Elizabeth Castillo * Swapna Behera
Tezmin Ition Tsai * William S. Peters, Sr.

The Year of the Poet IX
April 2022

Featured Global Poets
**Alonzo Gross * Dr. Debaprasanna Biswas
Monsif Beroual * Carol Aronoff**

Climate Change and Oceans

Celebrating our 100th Edition

Poetry . . . Ekphrasticly Speaking

The Poetry Posse 2021

Gail Weston Shazor * Albert Carasco * Hülya N. Yılmaz
Jackie Davis Allen * Caroline Nazareno * Eliza Segiet
Alicja Maria Kuberska * Teresa E. Gallion * Joe Paire
Kimberly Burnham * Shareef Abdur – Rasheed
Ashok K. Bhargava * Elizabeth Castillo * Swapna Behera
Tezmin Ition Tsai * William S. Peters, Sr.

Now Available
www.innerchildpress.com/the-year-of-the-poet

Inner Child Press Anthologies

The Year of the Poet IX
May 2022

Featured Global Poets
Ndaba Sibanda * Smrutiranjan Mohanty
Ajanta Paul * Monalisa Dash Dwibedy

Climate Change and Birds

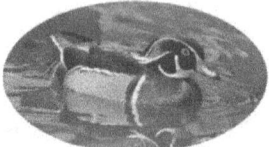

Poetry . . . Ekphrasticly Speaking

The Poetry Posse 2021

Gail Weston Shazor * Albert Carasco * Hülya N. Yılmaz
Jackie Davis Allen * Caroline Nazareno * Eliza Segiet
Alicja Maria Kuberska * Teresa E. Gallion * Joe Paire
Kimberly Burnham * Shareef Abdur – Rasheed
Ashok K. Bhargava * Elizabeth Castillo * Swapna Behera
Tezmin Ition Tsai * William S. Peters, Sr.

The Year of the Poet IX
June 2022

Featured Global Poets
Yuan Changming * Azeezat Okunlola
Tanja Ajtić * Philip Chijioke Abonyi

Climate Change and Trees

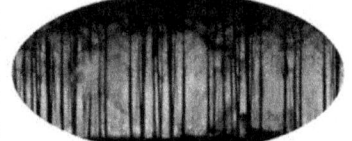

Poetry . . . Ekphrasticly Speaking

The Poetry Posse 2022

Gail Weston Shazor * Albert Carasco * Hülya N. Yılmaz
Jackie Davis Allen * Caroline Nazareno * Eliza Segiet
Alicja Maria Kuberska * Teresa E. Gallion * Joe Paire
Kimberly Burnham * Shareef Abdur – Rasheed
Ashok K. Bhargava * Elizabeth Castillo * Swapna Behera
Tezmin Ition Tsai * William S. Peters, Sr.

The Year of the Poet IX
July 2022

Featured Global Poets
**Michelle Joan Barulich * Mili Das
Anna Ferriero * Ujjal Mandal**

Climate Change and Animals

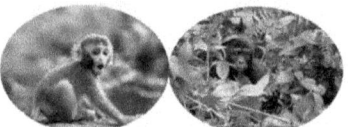

Poetry . . . Ekphrasticly Speaking

The Poetry Posse 2022

Gail Weston Shazor * Albert Carasco * Hülya N. Yılmaz
Jackie Davis Allen * Caroline Nazareno * Eliza Segiet
Alicja Maria Kuberska * Teresa E. Gallion * Joe Paire
Kimberly Burnham * Shareef Abdur – Rasheed
Ashok K. Bhargava * Elizabeth Castillo * Swapna Behera
Tezmin Ition Tsai * William S. Peters, Sr.

The Year of the Poet IX
August 2022

Featured Global Poets
**Pankhuri Sinha * Abdulloh Abdumominov
Caroline Turunç * Tali Cohen Shabtai**

Climate Change and Agriculture

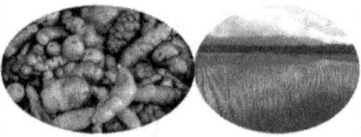

Poetry . . . Ekphrasticly Speaking

The Poetry Posse 2022

Gail Weston Shazor * Albert Carasco * Hülya N. Yılmaz
Jackie Davis Allen * Caroline Nazareno * Eliza Segiet
Alicja Maria Kuberska * Teresa E. Gallion * Joe Paire
Kimberly Burnham * Shareef Abdur – Rasheed
Ashok K. Bhargava * Elizabeth Castillo * Swapna Behera
Tezmin Ition Tsai * William S. Peters, Sr.

Now Available

www.innerchildpress.com/the-year-of-the-poet

Inner Child Press Anthologies

The Year of the Poet IX
September 2022

Featured Global Poets
Ngozi Olivia Osuoha * Biswajit Mishra
Sylwia K. Malinowska * Sajid Hussein

Climate Change and Wind and Weather Patterns

Poetry . . . Ekphrasticly Speaking

The Poetry Posse 2022
Gail Weston Shazor * Albert Carasco * Hülya N. Yilmaz
Jackie Davis Allen * Caroline Nazareno * Eliza Segiet
Alicja Maria Kuberska * Teresa E. Gallion * Joe Paire
Kimberly Burnham * Shareef Abdur – Rasheed
Ashok K. Bhargava * Elizabeth Castillo * Swapna Behera
Tezmin Ition Tsai * William S. Peters, Sr.

The Year of the Poet IX
October 2022

Featured Global Poets
Andrew Kouroupos * Brenda Mohammed
Carthornia Kouroupos * Faleeha Hassan

Climate Change and Oil and Power

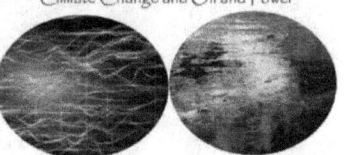

Poetry . . . Ekphrasticly Speaking

The Poetry Posse 2022
Gail Weston Shazor * Albert Carasco * Hülya N. Yilmaz
Jackie Davis Allen * Caroline Nazareno * Eliza Segiet
Alicja Maria Kuberska * Teresa E. Gallion * Joe Paire
Kimberly Burnham * Shareef Abdur – Rasheed
Ashok K. Bhargava * Elizabeth Castillo * Swapna Behera
Tezmin Ition Tsai * William S. Peters, Sr.

The Year of the Poet IX
November 2022

Featured Global Poets
Hema Ravi * Shafkat Aziz Hajam
Selma Kopic * Ibrahim Honjo

Climate Change : Time to Act

Poetry . . . Ekphrasticly Speaking

The Poetry Posse 2022
Gail Weston Shazor * Albert Carasco * Hülya N. Yilmaz
Jackie Davis Allen * Caroline Nazareno * Eliza Segiet
Alicja Maria Kuberska * Teresa E. Gallion * Joe Paire
Kimberly Burnham * Shareef Abdur – Rasheed
Ashok K. Bhargava * Elizabeth Castillo * Swapna Behera
Tezmin Ition Tsai * William S. Peters, Sr.

The Year of the Poet IX
December 2022

Featured Global Poets
Elarbi Abdelfattah * Lorraine Cragg
Neha Bhandarkar * Robert Gibbons

Climate Change Bees, Butterflies and Insect Life

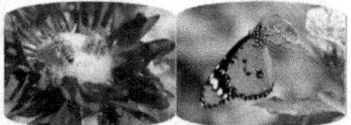

Poetry . . . Ekphrasticly Speaking

The Poetry Posse 2022
Gail Weston Shazor * Albert Carasco * Hülya N. Yilmaz
Jackie Davis Allen * Caroline Nazareno * Eliza Segiet
Alicja Maria Kuberska * Teresa E. Gallion * Joe Paine
Kimberly Burnham * Shareef Abdur – Rasheed
Ashok K. Bhargava * Elizabeth Castillo * Swapna Behera
Tezmin Ition Tsai * William S. Peters, Sr.

Now Available
www.innerchildpress.com/the-year-of-the-poet

Inner Child Press Anthologies

The Year of the Poet X
January 2023

Featured Global Poets

JuNe Barefield * Swayam Prashant
Willow Rose * Shabbirhusein K Jamnagerwalla

Children : Difference Makers

Iqbal Masih

The Poetry Posse 2023

Gail Weston Shazor * Albert Carasso * Hülya N. Yılmaz
Jackie Davis Allen * Caroline Nazareno * Kimberly Burnham
Alicja Maria Kuberska * Teresa E. Gallion * Joe Paire
Michelle Joan Barulich * Shareef Abdur – Rasheed
Ashok K. Bhargava * Elizabeth Castillo * Swapna Behera
Tezmin Ition Tsai * Eliza Segiet * William S. Peters, Sr.

The Year of the Poet X
February 2023

Featured Global Poets

Christena Williams * Hilda Graciela Kraft
Francesco Favetta * Dr. H.C. Louise Hudon

Children : Difference Makers

Ruby Bridges

The Poetry Posse 2023

Gail Weston Shazor * Albert Carasso * Hülya N. Yılmaz
Jackie Davis Allen * Caroline Nazareno * Kimberly Burnham
Alicja Maria Kuberska * Teresa E. Gallion * Joe Paire
Michelle Joan Barulich * Shareef Abdur – Rasheed
Ashok K. Bhargava * Elizabeth Castillo * Swapna Behera
Tezmin Ition Tsai * Eliza Segiet * William S. Peters, Sr.

The Year of the Poet X
March 2023

Featured Global Poets

Clarena Martínez Turizo * Binod Dawadi
Til Kumari Sharma * Petrouchka Alexieva

Children : Difference Makers

Yo Yo Ma

The Poetry Posse 2023

Gail Weston Shazor * Albert Carasso * Hülya N. Yılmaz
Jackie Davis Allen * Caroline Nazareno * Kimberly Burnham
Alicja Maria Kuberska * Teresa E. Gallion * Joe Paire
Michelle Joan Barulich * Shareef Abdur – Rasheed
Ashok K. Bhargava * Elizabeth Castillo * Swapna Behera
Tezmin Ition Tsai * Eliza Segiet * William S. Peters, Sr.

The Year of the Poet X
April 2023

Featured Global Poets

Maxwanette A Poetess * Alonzo Gross
Türkan Ergör * Ibrahim Honjo

Children : Difference Makers

Claudette Colvin

The Poetry Posse 2023

Gail Weston Shazor * Albert Carasso * Hülya N. Yılmaz
Jackie Davis Allen * Caroline Nazareno * Kimberly Burnham
Alicja Maria Kuberska * Teresa E. Gallion * Joe Paire
Michelle Joan Barulich * Shareef Abdur – Rasheed
Ashok K. Bhargava * Elizabeth Castillo * Swapna Behera
Tezmin Ition Tsai * Eliza Segiet * William S. Peters, Sr.

Now Available

www.innerchildpress.com/the-year-of-the-poet

Inner Child Press Anthologies

Now Available
www.innerchildpress.com/the-year-of-the-poet

Inner Child Press Anthologies

The Year of the Poet X
September 2023

Featured Global Poets
Eftichia Kapadeli * Chinh Nguyen
Nigar Agalarova * Carmela Cueva

Children : Difference Makers

~ Easton LaChappelle ~
The Poetry Posse 2023

Gail Weston Shazor * Albert Carasco * Hülya N. Yılmaz
Jackie Davis Allen * Caroline Nazareno * Kimberly Burnham
Alicja Maria Kuberska * Teresa E. Gallion * Joe Paire
Michelle Joan Barulich * Shareef Abdur – Rasheed
Ashok K. Bhargava * Elizabeth Castillo * Swapna Behera
Tezmin Ition Tsai * Eliza Segiet * William S. Peters, Sr.

The Year of the Poet X
October 2023

Featured Global Poets
CSP Shrivastava * Huniie Parker
Noreen Snyder * Ramkrishna Paul

Children : Difference Makers

~ Malala Yousafzai ~
The Poetry Posse 2023

Gail Weston Shazor * Albert Carasco * Hülya N. Yılmaz
Jackie Davis Allen * Caroline Nazareno * Kimberly Burnham
Alicja Maria Kuberska * Teresa E. Gallion * Joe Paire
Michelle Joan Barulich * Shareef Abdur – Rasheed
Ashok K. Bhargava * Elizabeth Castillo * Swapna Behera
Tezmin Ition Tsai * Eliza Segiet * William S. Peters, Sr.

The Year of the Poet X
November 2023

Featured Global Poets
Ibrahim Honjo * Balachandran Nair
Xanthi Hondrou-Hil * Francesco Favetta

Children : Difference Makers

~ Jean-Michel Basquiat ~
The Poetry Posse 2023

Gail Weston Shazor * Albert Carasco * Hülya N. Yılmaz
Jackie Davis Allen * Caroline Nazareno * Kimberly Burnham
Alicja Maria Kuberska * Teresa E. Gallion * Joe Paire
Michelle Joan Barulich * Shareef Abdur – Rasheed
Ashok K. Bhargava * Elizabeth Castillo * Swapna Behera
Tezmin Ition Tsai * Eliza Segiet * William S. Peters, Sr.

The Year of the Poet X
December 2023

Featured Global Poets
Caroline Laurent Turunc * Neha Bhandarkar
Shafkat Aziz Hajam * Elarbi Abdelfattah

Children : Difference Makers

~ Melati and Isabel Wijsen ~
The Poetry Posse 2023

Gail Weston Shazor * Albert Carasco * Hülya N. Yılmaz
Jackie Davis Allen * Caroline Nazareno * Kimberly Burnham
Alicja Maria Kuberska * Teresa E. Gallion * Joe Paire
Michelle Joan Barulich * Shareef Abdur – Rasheed
Ashok K. Bhargava * Elizabeth Castillo * Swapna Behera
Tezmin Ition Tsai * Eliza Segiet * William S. Peters, Sr.

Now Available

www.innerchildpress.com/the-year-of-the-poet

Inner Child Press Anthologies

The Year of the Poet XI
January 2024

Featured Global Poets
Til Kumari Sharma * Shafkat Aziz Hajam
Daniela Marian * Eleni Vassiliou – Asteroskon

Renowned Poets

~ Phyllis Wheatley ~

The Poetry Posse 2024

Gail Weston Shazor * Albert Carasso * Hülya N. Yılmaz
Jackie Davis Allen * Caroline Nazareno * Mutawaf Shaheed
Alicja Maria Kuberska * Teresa E. Gallion * Noreen Snyder
Michelle Joan Barulich * Shareef Abdur – Rasheed
Ashok K. Bhargava * Elizabeth Castillo * Swapna Behera
Tezmin Ition Tsai * Eliza Segiet * William S. Peters, Sr.

The Year of the Poet XI
February 2024

Featured Global Poets
Caroline Laurent Turunç * Julio Pavanetti
Lidia Chiarelli * Lina Buividavičiūtė

Renowned Poets

~ Omar Khayyam ~

The Poetry Posse 2024

Gail Weston Shazor * Albert Carasso * Hülya N. Yılmaz
Jackie Davis Allen * Caroline Nazareno * Mutawaf Shaheed
Alicja Maria Kuberska * Teresa E. Gallion * Noreen Snyder
Michelle Joan Barulich * Shareef Abdur – Rasheed
Ashok K. Bhargava * Elizabeth Castillo * Swapna Behera
Tezmin Ition Tsai * Eliza Segiet * William S. Peters, Sr.

The Year of the Poet XI
March 2024

Featured Global Poets
Francesco Favetta * Jagjit Singh Zandu
Carmela Núñez Yukimura Peruana * Michael Lee Johnson

Renowned Poets

~ Nâzim Hikmet ~

The Poetry Posse 2024

Gail Weston Shazor * Albert Carasso * Hülya N. Yılmaz
Jackie Davis Allen * Caroline Nazareno * Mutawaf Shaheed
Alicja Maria Kuberska * Teresa E. Gallion * Noreen Snyder
Michelle Joan Barulich * Shareef Abdur – Rasheed
Ashok K. Bhargava * Elizabeth Castillo * Swapna Behera
Tezmin Ition Tsai * Eliza Segiet * William S. Peters, Sr.

The Year of the Poet XI
April 2024

Featured Global Poets
Hassanal Abdullah * Johny Takkedasila
Rajashree Mohapatra * Shirley Smothers

Renowned Poets

~ William Butler Yeats ~

The Poetry Posse 2024

Gail Weston Shazor * Albert Carasso Hülya N. Yılmaz
Jackie Davis Allen * Caroline Nazareno * Mutawaf Shaheed
Alicja Maria Kuberska * Teresa E. Gallion * Noreen Snyder
Michelle Joan Barulich * Shareef Abdur – Rasheed
Ashok K. Bhargava * Elizabeth Castillo * Swapna Behera
Tezmin Ition Tsai * Eliza Segiet * William S. Peters, Sr.

Now Available
www.innerchildpress.com/the-year-of-the-poet

Inner Child Press Anthologies

The Year of the Poet XI — May 2024

Featured Global Poets
Binod Dawadi * Petros Kyriakou Veloudas
Rayees Ahmad Kumar * Solomon C Jatta

Renowned Poets

~ Makhanlal Chaturvedi ~

The Poetry Posse 2024
Gail Weston Shazor * Albert Carasco * Hülya N. Yılmaz
Jackie Davis Allen * Caroline Nazareno * Mutawaf Shaheed
Alicja Maria Kuberska * Teresa E. Gallion * Noreen Snyder
Michelle Joan Barulich * Shareef Abdur – Rasheed
Ashok K. Bhargava * Elizabeth Castillo * Swapna Behera
Tezmin Ition Tsai * Eliza Segiet * William S. Peters, Sr.

The Year of the Poet XI — June 2024

Featured Global Poets
C. S. P Shrivastava * Maria Evelyn Quilla Soleta
Moulay Cherif Chebihi Hassani * Swayam Prashant

Renowned Poets

~ Langston Hughs ~

The Poetry Posse 2024
Gail Weston Shazor * Albert Carasco * Hülya N. Yılmaz
Jackie Davis Allen * Caroline Nazareno * Mutawaf Shaheed
Alicja Maria Kuberska * Teresa E. Gallion * Noreen Snyder
Michelle Joan Barulich * Shareef Abdur – Rasheed
Ashok K. Bhargava * Elizabeth Castillo * Swapna Behera
Tezmin Ition Tsai * Eliza Segiet * William S. Peters, Sr.

The Year of the Poet XI — July 2024

Featured Global Poets
Barbara Gaiardoni * Bharati Nayak
Errol Bean * Michael Lee Johnson

Renowned Poets

~ Pablo Neruda ~

The Poetry Posse 2024
Gail Weston Shazor * Albert Carasco * Hülya N. Yılmaz
Jackie Davis Allen * Caroline Nazareno * Mutawaf Shaheed
Alicja Maria Kuberska * Teresa E. Gallion * Noreen Snyder
Michelle Joan Barulich * Shareef Abdur – Rasheed
Ashok K. Bhargava * Elizabeth Castillo * Swapna Behera
Tezmin Ition Tsai * Eliza Segiet * William S. Peters, Sr.

The Year of the Poet XI — August 2024

Featured Global Poets
Ibrahim Honjo * Khalice Jade
Irma Kurti * Mennadi Farah

Renowned Poets

~ Li Bai ~

The Poetry Posse 2024
Gail Weston Shazor * Albert Carasco * Hülya N. Yılmaz
Jackie Davis Allen * Caroline Nazareno * Mutawaf Shaheed
Alicja Maria Kuberska * Teresa E. Gallion * Noreen Snyder
Michelle Joan Barulich * Shareef Abdur – Rasheed
Ashok K. Bhargava * Elizabeth Castillo * Swapna Behera
Tezmin Ition Tsai * Eliza Segiet * William S. Peters, Sr.

Now Available

www.innerchildpress.com/the-year-of-the-poet

Inner Child Press Anthologies

The Year of the Poet XI
September 2024

Featured Global Poets
Ngozi Olivia Osuoha * Teodozja Świderska
Chinh Nguyen * Awatef El Idrissi Boukhris

Renowned Poets

~ William Ernest Henley ~
The Poetry Posse 2024

Gail Weston Shazor * Albert Carasco * Hülya N. Yılmaz
Jackie Davis Allen * Caroline Nazareno * Mutawaf Shaheed
Alicja Maria Kuberska * Teresa E. Gallion * Noreen Snyder
Michelle Joan Barulich * Shareef Abdur – Rasheed
Ashok K. Bhargava * Elizabeth Castillo * Swapna Behera
Tzemin Ition Tsai * Eliza Segiet * William S. Peters, Sr.

The Year of the Poet XI
October 2024

Featured Global Poets
Deepak Kumar Dey * Shallal 'Anouz
Adnan Al-Sayegh * Taghrid Bou Merhi

Renowned Poets

~ Adam Mickiewicz ~
The Poetry Posse 2024

Gail Weston Shazor * Albert Carasco * Hülya N. Yılmaz
Jackie Davis Allen * Caroline Nazareno * Mutawaf Shaheed
Alicja Maria Kuberska * Teresa E. Gallion * Noreen Snyder
Michelle Joan Barulich * Shareef Abdur – Rasheed
Ashok K. Bhargava * Elizabeth Castillo * Swapna Behera
Tzemin Ition Tsai * Eliza Segiet * William S. Peters, Sr.

The Year of the Poet XI
November 2024

Featured Global Poets
Abraham Tawiah Tei * Neha Bhandarkar
Zaneta Varnado Johns * Haseena Bnaiyan

Renowned Poets

~ Wole Soyinka ~
The Poetry Posse 2024

Gail Weston Shazor * Albert Carasco * Hülya N. Yılmaz
Jackie Davis Allen * Caroline Nazareno * Mutawaf Shaheed
Alicja Maria Kuberska * Teresa E. Gallion * Noreen Snyder
Michelle Joan Barulich * Shareef Abdur – Rasheed
Ashok K. Bhargava * Elizabeth Castillo * Swapna Behera
Tzemin Ition Tsai * Eliza Segiet * William S. Peters, Sr.

The Year of the Poet XI
December 2024

Featured Global Poets
Kapardeli Eftichia * Irena Jovanović
Sudipta Mishra * Til Kumari Sharma

Renowned Poets

~ Imru' al-Qais ~
The Poetry Posse 2024

Gail Weston Shazor * Albert Carasco * Hülya N. Yılmaz
Jackie Davis Allen * Caroline Nazareno * Mutawaf Shaheed
Alicja Maria Kuberska * Teresa E. Gallion * Noreen Snyder
Michelle Joan Barulich * Shareef Abdur – Rasheed * Swapna Behera
Ashok K. Bhargava * Elizabeth Castillo * Kimberly Burnham
Tzemin Ition Tsai * Eliza Segiet * William S. Peters, Sr.

Now Available

www.innerchildpress.com/the-year-of-the-poet

Inner Child Press Anthologies

The Year of the Poet XII
January 2025

Featured Global Poets

Khalice Jade * Til Kumari Sharma
Sushant Thapa * Orbindu Ganga

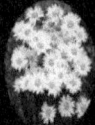 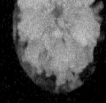 

| Innocence | Joy | Longing |
| Daisy | Marigold | Camellia |

The Poetry Posse 2025

Gail Weston Shazor * Albert Carasco * Hülya N. Yılmaz
Jackie Davis Allen * Caroline Nazareno * Mutawaf Shaheed
Alicja Maria Kuberska * Teresa E. Gallion * Noreen Snyder
Shareef Abdur – Rasheed * Swapna Behera * Eliza Segiet
Ashok K. Bhargava * Elizabeth Castillo * Kimberly Burnham
Tzemin Ition Tsai * William S. Peters, Sr.

The Year of the Poet XII
February 2025

Featured Global Poets

Shafkat Aziz Hajam * Frosina Tasevska
Muhammad Gaddafi Masoud * Karen Morrison

 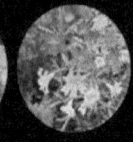 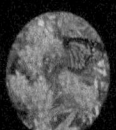

| Curiosity | Fear | Lonliness |
| Hibiscus | Minulus | Butterfly Weed |

The Poetry Posse 2025

Gail Weston Shazor * Albert Carasco * Hülya N. Yılmaz
Jackie Davis Allen * Caroline Nazareno * Mutawaf Shaheed
Alicja Maria Kuberska * Teresa E. Gallion * Noreen Snyder
Shareef Abdur – Rasheed * Swapna Behera * Eliza Segiet
Ashok K. Bhargava * Elizabeth Castillo * Kimberly Burnham
Tzemin Ition Tsai * William S. Peters, Sr.

The Year of the Poet XII
March 2025

Featured Global Poets

Deepak Kumar Dey * Binod Dawadi
Faleeha Hassan * Kapardeli Eftichia

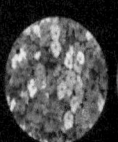  

| Frustration | Sorrow | Detrmination |
| Petunias | Purple Hyacinth | Amaryllis |

The Poetry Posse 2025

Gail Weston Shazor * Albert Carasco * Hülya N. Yılmaz
Jackie Davis Allen * Caroline Nazareno * Mutawaf Shaheed
Alicja Maria Kuberska * Teresa E. Gallion * Noreen Snyder
Shareef Abdur – Rasheed * Swapna Behera * Eliza Segiet
Ashok K. Bhargava * Elizabeth Castillo * Kimberly Burnham
Tzemin Ition Tsai * William S. Peters, Sr.

The Year of the Poet XII
April 2025

Featured Global Poets

Gopal Sinha * Taghrid Bou Merhi
Irma Kurti * Marlon Salem Gruezo

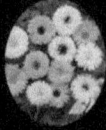  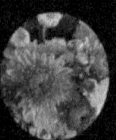

| Resilience | Self Doubt | Grief |
| Calendula | Centaury | Chrysanthemums |

The Poetry Posse 2025

Gail Weston Shazor * Albert Carasco * Hülya N. Yılmaz
Jackie Davis Allen * Caroline Nazareno * Mutawaf Shaheed
Alicja Maria Kuberska * Teresa E. Gallion * Noreen Snyder
Shareef Abdur – Rasheed * Swapna Behera * Eliza Segiet
Ashok K. Bhargava * Elizabeth Castillo * Kimberly Burnham
Tzemin Ition Tsai * William S. Peters, Sr.

Now Available

www.innerchildpress.com/the-year-of-the-poet

and there is much, much more !

visit . . .

www.innerchildpress.com/anthologies-sales-special.php

Also check out our Authors and all the wonderful Books Available at :

www.innerchildpress.com/authors-pages

Inner Child Press Anthologies

Now Available

www.worldhealingworldpeacepoetry.com

Inner Child Press Anthologies

Now Available

www.worldhealingworldpeacepoetry.com

Inner Child Press Anthologies

Now Available

www.worldhealingworldpeacepoetry.com

Inner Child Press Anthologies

Now Available

www.worldhealingworldpeacepoetry.com

World Healing World Peace
2012, 2014, 2016, 2018, 2020, 2022, 2024

Now Available

www.worldhealingworldpeacepoetry.com

Inner Child Press International

'building bridges of cultural understanding'

Meet the Board of Directors

William S. Peters, Sr.
Chair Person
Founder
Inner Child Enterprises
Inner Child Press

Hülya N Yılmaz
Director
Editing Services
Co-Chair Person

Fahredin B. Shehu
Director
Cultural Affairs

Elizabeth E. Castillo
Director
Recording Secretary

De'Andre Hawthorne
Director
Performance Poetry

Gail Weston Shazor
Director
Anthologies

Kimberly Burnham
Director
Cultural Ambassador
Pacific Northwest
USA

Ashok K. Bhargava
Director
WIN Awards

Deborah Smart
Director
Publicity
Marketing

Khalice Jade
Director
Translation
Services

www.innerchildpress.com

This Anthological Publication
is underwritten solely by

Inner Child Press International

Inner Child Press is a Publishing Company Founded and Operated by Writers. Our personal publishing experiences provides us an intimate understanding of the sometimes daunting challenges Writers, New and Seasoned may face in the Business of Publishing and Marketing their Creative "Written Work".

For more Information

Inner Child Press International

www.innerchildpress.com

'building bridges of cultural understanding'
202 Wiltree Court, State College, Pennsylvania 16801
www.innerchildpress.com

~ fini ~

www.ingramcontent.com/pod-product-compliance
Lightning Source LLC
LaVergne TN
LVHW051042080426
835508LV00019B/1661